BEYOND
THE
CORE

BEYOND
THE
CORE

Expand Your Market Without
Abandoning Your Roots

———

CHRIS ZOOK

Harvard Business School Press

Boston, Massachusetts

Copyright 2004 Bain & Company, Inc.
All rights reserved
Printed in the United States of America
08 07 06 05 04   5 4 3 2 1

Library of Congress Cataloging-in-Publication Data
Zook, Chris, 1951–
    Beyond the core : expand your market without abandoning your roots /
Chris Zook.
        p. cm.
    Includes bibliographical references and index.
    ISBN 1-57851-951-9 (alk. paper)
    1. Corporations—Growth. 2. Strategic planning. 3. Corporate profits.
    4. Industrial management. I. Title.

HD2746.Z657 2004
658.4'06—dc21

                                                            2003013374

Contents

Preface

The drive for growth has been fundamental to businesses for centuries. If businesses have a primal urge, it is the need for profitable growth. That growth is the source of value creation to shareholders. It is the gravitational pull that attracts and retains the best people. It is the life force of the organization. And it is the fuel to outpace competitors. No business that has failed to grow has ever been able to maintain excellence over time; this has always been true and probably always will be.

Yet, something has changed the game fundamentally, increasing the pressures to find growth more than ever before, raising to new levels the penalties for failure, and moving the goalposts of growth farther down the field. No other period in the history of business has seen as many economic disasters driven, in part, by the reckless pursuit of lofty growth objectives. One study my team conducted identified the twenty-five most costly business disasters from 1997 through 2002 (excluding those caused by the dot-com bubble). In 75 percent of the cases, the root cause, or a major contributing factor, was a failed growth strategy whose unrealized goal was to move profitably into new, adjacent areas surrounding a core business. At the same time, many of the great success stories of value creation or turnaround in the 1990s were cases of bold, new moves that successfully pushed out the business boundaries beyond the core. Some, like IBM, Li & Fung, and STMicroelectronics, are inspired stories of rejuvenation. Others, like Dell, Vodafone, and Nike, are stories of the relentless repeatability of a powerful growth engine.

I realized the potential for a book on the topic of how businesses push out the boundaries of their core businesses during a trip to Rio de Janeiro. It was my sixth talk in two days. I was reporting on some new research that we had conducted at Bain & Company on the sources of profitable growth. It was one of nearly two hundred such presentations in eighteen countries that I was privileged to make after the publication of my first book, *Profit from the Core*. The presentation contained data and analysis that argued that the most successful growth companies used every trick in the book to realize the full potential of their strongest businesses before venturing into potentially greener pastures outside their core. The talk cataloged case after case of companies that had abandoned their cores in search of new sources of profitable growth, only to realize that the greener pastures were not so green after all and that their departure from the core had been far too premature.

While the attendees in country after country liked and generally agreed with these ideas, they asked the same natural follow-up questions that seem so consistent with the heightened pressures businesses are feeling to grow.

"Yes," they would say, "full potential in the core business should be top priority, but what then? What if there really is not enough growth in my core business? What if I am a follower in my core business and want to build on my strengths to grow another way; is that possible? How have companies stuck in a niche taken their best skills and broken out into new territory successfully? What is the best way to balance focusing on my core business while also pushing into new, adjacent territory at the same time? How do I hedge growth bets at the periphery of my business without becoming too diffuse?"

Suddenly, I recognized the theme underlying these questions: What is similar to and different from growth at the boundaries of business, as opposed to growth right in the core? These questions triggered a new wave of research on the growth patterns of companies, focusing especially on the risks and benefits from extending the boundaries of a core business.

The primary original sources of information that I used for this book are these:

- One hundred company profiles and executive interviews, of which twenty-five were companies with some of the best growth records in the world (these companies are listed in the appendix). For these twenty-five, my colleagues and I conducted in-depth CEO interviews, other management interviews, and a complete company profile.

- Original analysis of twelve company pairs that were in similar situations in the early 1990s, but whose different expansion paths and choices led to dramatically different financial performance and strategic position (see appendix). Together, these twenty-four companies made more than five hundred growth moves from their core business; my team examined these different moves.

- A database of 181 major growth initiatives from 1995 to 1997 in the United States and the United Kingdom. For these initiatives, we did our best to assess their outcome and calculate the typical odds of success.

- The database built for *Profit from the Core.* These numbers include fourteen years of financial information for more than eight thousand public companies in seven major countries.

- Three special global surveys of executive perceptions and intentions about growth, conducted jointly by Bain & Company and the Economist Intelligence Unit.

Other sources tapped included my team's analysis of the odds of achieving profitable growth under different starting conditions, a full examination of the secondary data, access to the Bain & Company archives, and my notes from discussions at nearly two hundred business forums and events.

I believe that this is the first book-length study of such strategic adjacency moves and hope that three groups of readers will benefit from its findings: executives charged with making difficult choices about growth; boards of directors providing oversight on major new growth initiatives; and investors trying to understand the risks inherent in companies' strategies. A 2002 survey showed that 86 percent of executives placed finding the next wave of profitable growth in their top three priorities—and 43 percent placed it at number one.[1] Hopefully, the new data and the company experiences in this book will inform better decisions in this key area.

Profit from the Core was about the power of focus, the choice of focus, and the cost of losing focus in a business. The finding that, during the 1990s, only about 13 percent of companies worldwide achieved even a modest level of sustained and profitable growth surprised executive audiences and other readers. Furthermore, the discovery that nearly all the sustained-growth companies were built around one or two strong or dominant cores proved a powerful counterpoint to some of the hallmark disastrous diversifications and investments of the 1990s. The book was replete with stories of businesses that incorrectly assessed their core strengths and that sought growth in the wrong places. It featured cases from a wide range of businesses that prematurely abandoned their cores in search of hot new growth, only to experience severe erosion in their once-strong business in addition to the direct cost of failed growth initiatives. How managers defined their companies' sources of competitive advantage, the economic boundaries of their core, and where they could or should compete effectively, and then assessed the full potential of that core, was at the heart of many examples.

This book picks up where the first one left off. *Beyond the Core* focuses on the question of how to expand a core business into adjacent areas in a way that is profitable and contributes to the strategic objective of expanding, defending, or redefining the core business. If the first book asked "Who am I?" this book raises the even more challenging follow-on questions of "Where should I go? What should I be? How do I get there?"

The six chapters of this book are organized around six questions that proceed in a logical sequence, beginning with the environment and definition of what I mean by an *adjacency* as a way for businesses to grow. I end with some observations on the long-term potential of these strategies not just to grow, but to transform, a company's core over time:

- What are adjacencies, and how often do they succeed?

- What is the best way to decide which adjacencies to pursue?

- What are the characteristics and sources of the most lasting adjacency strategies?

- When do adjacencies make the most sense, and when are they a last resort?

- What are the most important organizational enablers and inhibitors to the success of new adjacency initiatives?

- How often do these types of strategies not only grow, but also transform, a company's core over time?

These are all substantial questions whose correct answers will vary by the specifics of a company's situation. The intention is certainly not to be encyclopedic or to present a universal solution. That would make no sense. Rather, the intention is to identify the most universal success factors and provide some ideas that management teams might find useful in improving the odds of an inherently risky undertaking.

Acknowledgments

My first debt of gratitude must go to the clients of Bain & Company, who allow my partners and me to participate on a daily basis on the front lines of businesses in virtually every industry around the world. It seems as if the job of a senior executive in business is becoming more complex, more risky, and more pressurized every day. I have immense respect for these men and women who remain in the arena creating the value that propels the world economy.

I also thank all my partners at Bain & Company, most of whom have contributed an idea, a contact, a reference, or encouragement to this effort. After the publication of my first book, *Profit from the Core,* I had the privilege of visiting nearly all the Bain offices and speaking to our teams. At every stop, I learned about new and interesting local companies, such as Olam in Singapore, AmBev in São Paulo, and Centex Homes in Dallas, that have subsequently provided much of the input for this book.

It is impossible for me not to acknowledge certain partners who have supported this book from its inception to the end through their ideas, their encouragement, or their willingness to slog through my manuscripts. On the other hand, it is difficult to draw the line for whom to mention by name and whom to reference as part of the group. John Donahoe, Bain's managing director, and Orit Gadiesh, Bain's chairman, have been supportive of this book and of the Bain Growth Project without fail. Phyllis Yale, head of Bain's Northeast offices, supported the project by allowing me access to analytic resources, to time, and to her great judgment. As he did for the first book, Steve Schaubert read and commented in detail on every draft and has constantly encouraged me. I have collaborated with Darrell Rigby on a number of projects related to growth, including some work on innovation. There is no one more generous with his friendship, his ideas, and his time than Darrell. Jimmy Allen, my coauthor on the first book, has commented in detail on multiple drafts and worked closely with me on a myriad of other endeavors since then.

I also thank Chuck Farkas and Fred Reichheld for commenting on my earliest drafts. Mike Garstka gave me consistently good ideas, data, and advice regarding how the findings of this work applied to Asian companies. Wendy Miller, Cheryl Krauss, and the Bain marketing team were constantly by my side helping me to think through how best to articulate the key messages of the book.

At the core of this book are the insights from an extensive number of interviews, primarily of CEOs. I am deeply grateful to the executives who hosted me at their companies and told me their, and their companies', stories. These companies and the CEOs interviewed are listed in the appendix.

Marci Taylor has worked on the growth projects that have spawned both of my books from the very beginning. Without her competence, flexibility, judgment, and friendship, this book might have taken twice as long to be written and might have been half as accurate. Thank you.

In addition, I have been blessed with a continual stream of excellent Bain consultants on the notorious 3EC team. This group has generated more than a hundred modules of analysis on the topic of how companies grow and has codified at least as many case examples along the way. The Bain managers who have worked on this project, Ajay Agrawal, Emma Gray, David Fleisch, and Patrick O'Hagan, epitomize the best of Bain & Company.

Brenda Davis has prepared the manuscript, provided editorial help, scheduled the interviews, offered constant encouragement, injected needed humor and a sense of balance, and counseled me psychologically through the entire manuscript process. She has also somehow endured eight years as my assistant. I do not underestimate how much I owe to Brenda.

Melinda Adams Merino, my editor at Harvard Business School Press, has been my source of inspiration, my muse, my toughest coach, and my most constant adviser from concept to final manuscript. She has an uncanny sense of those few focused changes that, when complete, raise the product up a level. Melinda has also marshaled a fantastic team at Harvard on all the myriad dimensions, from cover design to format. Thank you.

Barbara Roth is the brilliant technical editor who worked on my first book and kindly agreed to provide me comments on this one, too, on her own time. Paul Judge at Bain read the manuscript and provided further insights at a key stage in the process.

Chip Baird, founder of Northcastle Partners, and Tom Meredith, former CFO of Dell, also read the manuscript and provided further powerful insight. Earl E. T. Smith Jr. has provided inspiration, important source material for the book, and a ready tennis game at critical junctures in the process, too.

The members of my family, particularly Donna, my wife of nearly three decades, have been saintlike in their patience and tolerance through the process of my giving birth to another book. My sons, Andrew and Alex, have been a continuous source of positive energy for everything I do.

BEYOND

THE

CORE

1

The Growth Crisis

Dangerous Moves Beyond the Core

Like an interminable tennis rally on the red clay of nearby Roland Garros, the verbal volleys flew across the table in the warm and crowded boardroom late that Paris afternoon. Back and forth went the heated argument about the new growth opportunity. Yes, the market research did show that the market could be enormous. But some tough competitors had already entered, so was it already too late? Yes, the finance department had documented a large profit gap that needed to be filled to meet investor promises. But was this really the most prudent place to make the big bet? Yes, the enthusiastic team was ready to launch the initiative. But had the members grown too close to it and lost their objectivity? The group ended the day inconclusively, tired and frustrated. They agreed to sleep on it and reconvene at 8 A.M. the next day. As he walked back to his office, the CEO felt enormous tension. The last few movements into adjacent markets in search of new growth had been disappointing. The core business was weakening and losing momentum. Was this risky proposal the answer? Or might it just exacerbate the problems, add complexity, and sap credibility? Was it worth the chance?

The Challenge for Today's CEOs

CEOs facing decisions about major investments in new growth initiatives that push out the boundaries of their core business into new territory ("adjacency moves") are often right to be concerned. While bold adjacency moves have proved for some to be the new well that liberates a gusher of growth, often that is not the case. When my team examined the top twenty-five business calamities (other than Internet companies) of the period 1997 to 2002, we concluded that a failed strategy to grow into a new adjacency around a once-successful core business was a critical factor in 75 percent of these disasters. Just consider the following examples of how a growth strategy can go awry:

- For nearly three decades, Loral and its CEO Bernard Schwartz represented the poster child for growth companies, expanding from a money loser in 1972, when Schwartz was hired, to the most successful defense electronics firm in the United States. To a *Wall Street Journal* reporter, Schwartz declared, "For thirty years of my life I walked on water."[1] Then in 1994, Loral made the first of several investments in Globalstar, a satellite-based mobile telephone system. The risky venture absorbed $1.8 billion of capital and a large share of management time in the ensuing years. When Globalstar collapsed in January 2001, defaulting on $3 billion of debt, Loral's stock price had declined 90 percent from the previous year.

- During the four years before becoming the largest bankruptcy in U.S. history, Enron moved into thirty-four different adjacencies around its core, five times more than in any previous decade. Many, such as investment in broadband futures, consulting, and water treatment, were far from their core. Many observers believe that the financial carnage and ethical issues were magnified by the operating disasters brought on by overzealous adjacency moves.

- Swissair had a seventy-year history of punctuality and attention to detail. Then, in 1995, a new management team decided to attempt a growth strategy that involved investments in ten regional airlines as well as in a series of services, from catering to maintenance. When the regional airlines began having financial difficulties, Swissair found that it had flown to an altitude it could not handle. Soon, Swissair's debt was five times its equity value and the company, having fired its management team and much of its board, was plummeting toward bankruptcy.

- In 2002, Wal-Mart became the largest company in the *Fortune* 500 and the most respected company in the United States, while Kmart drifted into bankruptcy. Both companies opened their first store in 1962. The history of Wal-Mart is one of methodical movement into adjacencies such as Sam's Club, and electronics, and Mexico, one by one. The history of Kmart is strewn with adjacency expansions gone wrong, from books (Walden) to sporting goods (Sports Authority) and even to a chain of department stores in Czechoslovakia. These failed adjacency moves sapped the strength of Kmart at exactly the time it was under a blistering attack to its core from one of the toughest competitors on earth.

These are extreme examples of what can happen when a growth strategy overreaches, pushing a company into spreading its resources too thin, or leaving its core unprotected, or moving into areas it simply doesn't know how to manage, or burdening the company with excessive risk. Yet, how did such smart management teams, all backed by market research, make these decisions while others hit the jackpot? Is it all good fortune, or is there something to be learned from the lessons of history?

Finding or maintaining a source of sustained and profitable growth has become the number one concern of most CEOs. And moves that push out the boundaries of their core business into "adjacencies" are where they are most often looking these days. As

Jack Welch commented regarding where he looked for growth within GE, "Expanding into adjacent businesses is the easiest way to grow. By challenging the organization to continually redefine their markets in a fashion that decreases their share opens their eyes to opportunities in adjacent markets."[2]

Profitable growth is the wellspring of most value creation in business. The prospect of achieving profitable growth provides the air under the wings of most companies' stock prices. The rewards of profitable growth offer a source of oxygen for employees at all levels. When profitable growth dies, these same forces of positive energy can begin to run in reverse, creating a downdraft, a reinforcing cycle, that can build a value-destroying momentum of their own.

When Jim Kilts, a veteran of some of the most successful turnarounds in the world of consumer products, took over the helm of Gillette in 2000, he referred to his number one priority of stopping the company's "self-inflicted cycle of death." Gillette had missed seventeen straight quarters of earnings targets, was starting to lose the edge of even its strongest core shaving business, and was seeing employee and investor confidence wane by the day. Kilts has since turned the company around, renewed confidence, and begun re-igniting growth. But what caused Gillette and similar companies to fall into this loss of profitable growth in the first place?

A mountain of economic evidence can be amassed (some presented throughout this book) to demonstrate that profitable growth is becoming increasingly elusive and more fleeting for most companies, not just Gillette. This was true during the boom times at the end of the 1990s, when even then, underlying corporate returns on capital were flagging in most industrialized countries. Profitable growth will probably be even more elusive during the first decade of the twenty-first century, a potential period of extended growth crisis worldwide.

There are myriad ways to grow a company—diversifying; investing in venture capital; accelerating the rate of innovation in R&D; grinding out hidden scraps of growth from deep inside the existing core business; jumping into new, hot markets; globalizing;

and stepping up the organization's "metabolism," getting it to work faster and thereby grow faster. Each of these methods has its zealous advocates. And in the right situation, each has some validity.

This book focuses on growth through adjacency strategies. These strategies have three distinctive features. First, they are of significant size, or they can lead to a sequence of related adjacency moves that generate substantial growth. Second, they build on, indeed are bolted on, a strong core business. Thus the adjacent area draws from the strengths of the core and at the same time may serve to reinforce or defend that core. Third, adjacency strategies are a journey into the unknown, a true extension of the core, a pushing-out of the boundaries, a step-up in risk from typical forms of organic growth.

Adjacency moves are typically made at the discretion of the CEO or the president of the relevant business unit and, by their nature, are among the most difficult decisions to make. They entail risk, potentially draw resources away from the core, and may shape the course of the future. Adjacency moves can be near the core, perhaps varying only one dimension, such as the decision to sell the same products to a totally new customer segment. These moves might also be much farther from the core. For example, the company might decide to sell a related product through a new channel against a poorly understood competitor. A recurring theme in this book is the importance of understanding the distance of a growth move from the core, one indicator of risk and movement into the unknown. We find that companies continually underestimate the amount that they do not understand, taking on risks and future obligations that are greater than they may have realized. Visually, you can think of this relationship as a set of concentric circles around the core, like the rings of a tree, radiating outward (figure 1-1).

The importance of understanding the true strength of the core to support new growth is a second theme that runs through this book. Again, we find that companies sometimes overestimate the ability of their core business to support new growth, or they see major adjacency moves as a way to leap to a new core, a new "lily

FIGURE 1 - 1

Growth Opportunities Should Be Examined Relative to a Core Business

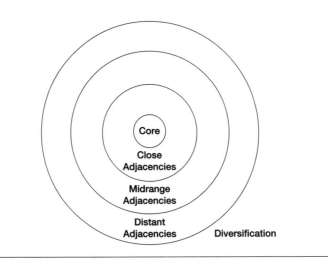

pad." The risks and benefits of such thinking are examined from a number of angles in later chapters.

An important theme of this book is what I refer to as "the new math of profitable growth." The most powerful long-term growth trajectories are composed of repeated sequences of smaller adjacency moves that lead to higher odds of success, the ability to handle many more initiatives at the same time, greater ability to anticipate and control the cost of failure, and the incentive to create a focused organization to implement these adjacencies that captures the learning and experience curve benefits of performing a similar task over and over. The arithmetic that accompanies such a "virtuous cycle" of growth becomes increasingly powerful over time. In contrast, the arithmetic that accompanies the occasional "big move" in search of growth embodies the opposite of all the positive factors listed above and seldom leads to sustained value creation.

What are successful adjacency moves, and why are they so important? An adjacency move could take many forms:

- *A shift from a flagging product business into services,* like the creation of IBM Global Services that rescued the company

- *A foray into a major new customer and product arena building on the strengths of a core business,* like the repeatable adjacency formula that Nike developed to enter sports, from running to basketball to golf

- *The leveraging of a core asset to create a totally new business,* like the creation of the Sabre reservation business by American Airlines

- *Migration into new geographic adjacencies,* like the string of acquisitions by Vodafone, which transformed that company from a small, local wireless operator in the United Kingdom to the world leader in cellular phone services

- *The addition of major new product lines to a distribution network,* like the Lloyds Bank strategy of applying retail techniques to its branch bank network, thereby adding products from mortgages to insurance, and reversing its position from one of the worst to one of the best performing banks in the world

The risks and potential value of entering the unknown, like the aforementioned companies did, are high. As much as 50 percent of the value of many stocks is based on investor expectations of future growth from unproven adjacency expansions around a core business. Diminished investor beliefs in a company's ability to grow can make this perceived value melt like wax.

The CEOs interviewed for this project commented frequently on the difficulty of formulating the right strategies for successful adjacency growth. As Jim Vincent, former CEO of Biogen, a leading biotechnology company, puts it, "Deciding when and how to push a core business into new adjacencies is the toughest decision faced by the CEO."[3] Tom Stemberg, founder and chairman of Staples, the leading office products retailer, agrees: "Adjacency expansion is one of the two toughest decisions I faced as a CEO, the other being the creation and retention of the best possible management team."[4]

The promise of this book is threefold. The first aim is to provide objective data to assess the odds and risks of adjacency moves under different circumstances. Executives need to better understand what they are getting into. Second, I have tried to provide a practical, battle-tested framework for identifying and then evaluating adjacency moves. Much of this background is based on statistical analysis; even more is based on a rich collection of my interviews and discussions with more than a hundred CEOs in conjunction with my Bain & Company partners all over the world. Third and finally, I present some ways to prepare an organization to accept, embrace, and fuel the new source of profitable growth.

STMicroelectronics: Rebuilding the Company Through Adjacencies

The resurrection of STMicroelectronics is a parable that encapsulates the patterns and ideas explored more extensively in this book. In 1980, Pasquale Pistorio agreed to leave his job as general manager of the International Semiconductor Division of Motorola to return to Italy to become CEO of the SGS Group, Italy's only microprocessor company. He walked into a small, government-owned company that was losing nearly fifty cents for every dollar of revenues and that was under attack from every direction up and down its product line. Just twenty-two years later, SGS, renamed STMicroelectronics, had become a $6.3 billion company, with $429 million in profits. It is one of the top five in the worldwide rankings led by Intel—microprocessing being a tough neighborhood in which to survive, let alone prosper—and the first non-U.S. company to win the Malcolm Baldrige Award. ST's story epitomizes the nature of adjacency expansion, building and then pushing out the boundaries of strong core businesses. Pistorio describes what he found when he first took over the helm:

It was a small company of $100 million that had been losing money for ten years and was owned by the Italian government. This was one-tenth the size of the business I had left in Motorola. But in spite of size differences, the product line was more than ten times broader than Motorola's. It included everything: DRAM [dynamic RAM], static RAM, EPROM [erasable programmable read-only memory], power transistors, integrated circuits, and on and on. It was like a big R&D center with nothing coming out that was being attacked in every direction. We immediately set about to shrink down to a few strong cores to focus resources so that we could build around products in which we had some competitive advantage and in customers that we thought could be good long-term partners.

You must create a dream and show the people it is possible. That is the job of the CEO. At the time, we said there were three major challenges. The first was to become profitable. The second was to sell and prove ourselves in the toughest market, the United States, which we had not entered. The third was to achieve scale and become part of the billion-dollar club. Some said there was no chance.

We decided to grow only in the products where we had clear competitive advantage. So we cut 80 percent of the products right away. We killed whole categories like DRAM and static RAM memories where competition was too strong or the level of investment needed was too high.

Sometimes you get lucky, and we did find a few nice technologies to build around. Those are the core technologies that have driven our growth into adjacent areas over and over, up to even today. One was power management. One was video compression. One was EPROM memories. One was the early technology in smart cards. These, plus some later additions like flash memory, gave us a lead in having all of the elements to produce customized systems on chip products that make up most of our sales and more of our profits today.

We also needed scale. So, in 1986, we combined with another company in distress, Thompson Semiconducteurs of France, which was losing $200 million per year. I believed that we could build one good company from these two troubled companies.[5]

Once ST had, in fact, achieved scale and profitability built around Pistorio's four core technologies, it began to expand into adjacencies:

Our intention was to find even small parts of key customer segments where we could become number one in the world. We went to telecom and said, in wired [segments of telecommunications] it is too late, but in parts of wireless it is not. Power management is among the most important functions for handsets, and there we did have leading technology. So, today we are the leading supplier to Nokia, one of our most important strategic alliance customers, and we are probably the only company capable of supplying all the chips—from smart cards to video cameras—that are needed for a complete cell phone solution that can drive the entire phone. Computers were the second segment. We said we did not want to do DRAM and did not want to challenge Intel. That led us to peripherals like printers, and monitors, and disk drives where we are number one now. Consumer was another segment. We picked some areas of consumer digital and focused there, and we are now number one in the set-top box. Smart card is another area where we focused and are now number two. Though we are a world leader, we have only 4.5 percent share of the overall semiconductor market. When people say, let's do other things, I say no. There is plenty of room to go in and around our current cores. If we moved into another area, I would ask why. We would need to have a proprietary competitive advantage, plus there is plenty to do here.

ST is essentially organized around the customer, the source of the company's best growth ideas. Pistorio is in close personal touch, almost as a coach or mentor, with all his key account managers who serve ST's largest customers. These deep customer relationships have allowed ST to expand. In 2003, thirty customers constituted 65 percent of the business, and twelve of these thirty constituted 45 percent and an even larger part of the growth.

Pistorio underscores the importance of the customer relationship:

> We are totally devoted to serving our key customers. They stimulate nearly all of our insights for new growth. I have regular meetings with each account executive and visit the strategic partners in person several times a year. The only way I know how to manage is by traveling to the customer. I travel most of the time, and most of that time is spent visiting customers. Receiving reports is nice, but you have to sit in front of your customer and have them say you did a great job or you must improve. If we listen and perform, they reward us with growth. I am a salesman. I was born one. I am still a pretty good salesman. The customer's decision to give me some of his purchasing power is what makes me successful or not. You must be humble as well as take pride in your own knowledge. Most of the new adjacencies we have gone after have been driven by what we learned from the customers. Our biggest adjacency disappointments have been ones like a chip for PCs or a graphics chip that were not driven by the customer.

One theme throughout this book is the repeatability of adjacency strategies. A diagram of ST's growth would show a pattern in which the company enters a new technology in response to insights from ST's core twelve customers, applies that technology to new customer segments, then expands it into new geographic areas, and starts the cycle again. ST tops its industry in terms of R&D spending as a percentage of sales at 15.4 percent. And more than 95 percent of the R&D budget goes to developing new capabilities for existing customers rather than making bets on the future in general.

ST's record contrasts strikingly with the travails of Advanced Micro Devices (AMD), the U.S. semiconductor manufacturer. ST and AMD had remarkably similar financial situations at the time of ST's initial public offering (IPO) in 1994:

	ST	AMD
Revenues	$2.6 billion	$2.1 billion
Net income	$362 million	$305 million
Market value	$2.9 billion	$2.4 billion
Share price, Dec. 1994	$3.78	$12.62
Share price, Jan. 2003	$20.11	$5.04
Share price gain	+532%	(60)%

While companies like Intel and ST were narrowing their focus in the late 1980s to achieve leadership in a segment, AMD remained in memory chips as well as semiconductors, fighting on a broad front and achieving dominance nowhere. As a result of that strategy, AMD created no shareholder value during the 1990s. While ST's stock price almost quintupled, despite the semiconductor market slump, AMD's stock fell dramatically over this same period. Two companies with similar financial starting points in 1994 had dramatically different management decisions and outcomes.

The STMicroelectronics story reveals three truths that reappeared over and over in our study. First, adjacency expansion is successful only if built around the strongest cores that have potential for leadership economics. Second, the best adjacency expansion strategies have a repeatable characteristic allowing the company to build an adjacency machine that continually creates more growth opportunities of a similar nature. And finally, the best place to look for adjacency opportunities is in the strongest customers. It is not in the search for hot markets, the next big deal, or in corporate studies. Your customer's potential adjacencies become your own potential adjacencies. As Pistorio says, "The truth is at the customer. It is not in the office."

The Pressure of Growth Expectations

My first book, *Profit from the Core,* presented evidence based on studies of 1,870 companies followed over ten years. The research showed that only 13 percent of companies worldwide achieved even a modest level of sustained and profitable growth. This simple statistic held in most countries, from Germany to Brazil and even to many growing Asian markets. Most audiences to whom I spoke met the statistic with surprise and interest. Yet, the proportion of companies that achieve sustained and profitable growth will probably be lower in the next five years, and maybe longer. Still, investors, employees, and financial markets demand more and more growth, even as the target becomes harder to hit.

Since 1996, analyst forecasts of the long-term growth rate of companies in the Standard & Poor's (S&P) 500 index have called for an earnings growth of more than 12 percent on average. This level of expectation has hardly dropped, even during the extended recessionary period of the late 1990s to early 2000s. Yet, on average, the earnings of the S&P 500 have not kept up with the rate of growth of the U.S. economy since the 1960s, let alone hit a 12 percent level. Furthermore, the 13 percent figure cited in the preceding paragraph was based on companies that had grown earnings and revenues at a rate exceeding 5.5 percent (adjusted for inflation) and that had earned their cost of capital over ten years, on average. So, analysts are calling for average growth to far exceed the amount that even the best 13 percent of companies have achieved.

These growth expectations are built into stock prices in several ways. One telling way is through the average price-to-earnings ratios, which remain at a high level of 19 based on trailing operating earnings, and at an even higher level based on total earnings. No other recessionary period on record in the United States has seen such high stock valuations.

What, then, is driving stock price? To determine this, we analyzed the long-term cash flow projections for the profitable cores of many prominent companies, like Microsoft and The Home Depot. We then replicated this analysis in a number of foreign markets, such as the London Stock Exchange and the Asian stock markets. We found that the value of the core businesses, as measured by a discounted cash flow at their cost of capital, accounted for only about 50 to 65 percent of market value. So, where is the rest? The answer for companies like these, which are not takeover or breakup candidates, is that it must lie in future growth opportunities—either known adjacencies not yet fully developed or undiscovered adjacencies.

Take Microsoft. Our calculations suggest that about half of Microsoft's $356 billion market value could be accounted for by currently projectable cash flows of the existing, profitable core businesses. These core businesses, the operating system business for personal computers (Windows and NT) and the office productivity suite (Word, Excel), accounted for virtually 100 percent of the company's profitability in 2001—a percentage that has hardly changed since the early 1990s. As the growth of the personal computer market slows and the take-up rate of new software steadily decreases, Microsoft's management must come up with large sources of new, profitable growth. About half of the remaining core business valuation and the stock price, we calculate, comes from profit projections of known adjacencies such as video games. The remaining component, as much as 25 percent of stock price valuation, comes from future adjacencies not yet seen in the marketplace.

In a world where the average share of common stock is held by investors for only about nine months (as compared to nearly nine years in the 1970s), even the innuendo of slowed growth or a disappointment with a major new growth initiative can collapse stock values overnight. Just consider the 85 percent decline in stock price experienced by Gap after a wave of disappointing store openings, a season of merchandising mistakes, and slumping performance in its adjacency expansion initiatives abroad. Bear in mind that the ten-year performance of Gap before this collapse showed an average annual return to shareholders of 37 percent and an average annual growth rate of 22 percent. Moreover, this company enjoys a strong brand, a core of proven locations, and a once-proven formula relying not on fashion, but on basics.

This crisis of growth creates enormous pressures for companies to make visible growth moves. By screening headlines, analyzing financial data on stock and earnings declines, and looking at bankruptcy filings, we identified twenty-five of the most calamitous business disasters (non-Internet-related) from 1997 through 2002. In total, these twenty-five companies experienced an 88 percent loss in value, or $1.1 trillion. In about three-quarters of these cases, a failed expansion strategy into adjacencies was front and center stage. Examples include Enron's unfettered move into thirty-five adjacencies over four years, Loral's investment in the Globalstar system, and Mattel's purchase of The Learning Company.

Not surprisingly, we also found that more than 40 percent of nonretirement CEO turnover was in the presence of a major adjacency move that had gone wrong or that was highly controversial. The 2001–2002 period has been the highest on record for CEO turnover. Many analysts estimate that the average CEO's tenure in the United States and some European countries is now less than four years, barely time for an executive to develop and begin implementing a new agenda, never mind seeing strategies come to fruition. This combination of unrealistic growth expectations, increased difficulty in achieving growth, more volatile stock prices hinging on prospects of adjacency growth, and greater willingness to dismiss CEOs and their teams puts enormous pressure on managers trying to balance these forces while serving their customers day to day.

The Three Purposes of Adjacency Expansion

This discussion has focused on the pressures and dangers of growth. Yet, it is the rewards of success that drive energy and investment in business. And few types of initiatives, when successful, can be more powerful than a major adjacency expansion program. The following three cases show clearly how adjacency expansion can create a new wave of profitable growth for its own sake; can strengthen, reinforce, and even defend a core business; and can redefine a business facing turbulence in its market.

UPS: Expanding the Core Through Adjacencies

Walk into the Atlanta headquarters of UPS, the package delivery company, and look down. You will see floor tiles signifying countries all over the world, with UPS locations marked by a star. Look up, and you will see a quote from founder Jim Casey: "An expanding business is the only way to provide opportunities for our people." There are now nearly 360,000 of those people, a far cry from the ten-person bicycle messenger business Casey started in Seattle about one hundred years ago. By 2002, around a central core of delivery and in a market growing at 4 to 5 percent, UPS held a two-decade-long record that placed it among the most elite performing growth companies. From 1981 to 1991, UPS grew revenues from $4.9 billion to $15 billion and then kept on growing to $31.3 billion in 2002. From 1991 to 2001, with the surge in new information capabilities increasing efficiency, the company's profits expanded to $2.4 billion, a 17 percent annual growth rate. Since its IPO in 1999, UPS has outperformed the S&P 500 index by 40 percent—not bad for a company in a core business whose public image is a brown truck.

When CEO Mike Eskew talks about the shaping events in the history of UPS, he starts all the way back with the early years, recounting a series of adjacency moves that propelled the company forward again and again. In efficient fashion, like the UPS business itself, he ticks off the key transitions: from local message delivery (1907), to local package delivery (1918), to regional package delivery to common carrier (1950), to national network, to the addition of two-day air freight capabilities (1953), to next-day-air service through the purchase of a fleet of planes (1988), to global package delivery today by virtually any method. The next step is the new wave of specialized logistics and information adjacencies that represent the growth hope for the future.

As the network has expanded, and as information technologies have been added, the number of delivery options and adjacent products has proliferated. UPS has spawned almost a repeatable formula for discovering new adjacent customer needs ranging from service parts delivery and logistics to tracking services. For instance, the company sells its software and tracking abilities to Ford Motor Company so that the automaker can keep track of all of its vehicles from assembly to dealer. Since only 6 percent of supply-chain costs are transportation, this expanded way of defining the business has evolved, as Eskew says, to "enablers of global commerce."

An example of one adjacency is the service parts logistics business (described more fully in chapter 5), a UPS division that delivers, stores, tracks, and retrieves critical parts needed within two to four hours for equipment repair. UPS entered this business in 1995 with a small acquisition, studied the market in depth, and discovered that the acquisition held nearly ten times the potential UPS had originally recognized. UPS mobilized and built a business that rapidly approached $1 billion in revenues in 2002. Not a bad adjacency expansion. At the same time that UPS was entering these new adjacencies, it was starting to think of its core business in broader terms, moving from pure delivery to an expanded definition of logistics and the enablers of global commerce. From 1998 to 2003, these new initiatives in logistics and commerce accounted for more than half of the company's new growth. How, and how well, it pursues and executes this adjacency strategy will determine the trajectory in the next decade.

Li & Fung: Redefining the Core Through Adjacencies

Li & Fung, founded in 1906 in Canton, was one of the earliest Chinese-financed trading companies to engage in exports from China. The company's initial exports were porcelain, silk, jade, ivory, and fireworks. In 1937, because Hong Kong offered an advantage as a deepwater port, the company set up a branch at the port and eventually moved its headquarters operations there. With the growth of manufacturing in China, Li & Fung diversified further, into trading consumer goods ranging from electronics to export garments. Things were not going smoothly, however, when Victor and William Fung took over the company from their father in the 1970s. They found a business under pressure, with brokerage fees declining because Asian manufacturers were dealing directly with Western customers more and more. Victor describes the decline: "Under our grandfather, margins declined from 20 percent to 10 percent. Under our father, margins declined again to 5 percent, and as we took over and looked at the future, margins were dropping well below that. We knew we had to do something."[6]

They recognized that simply trading finished goods was not a sustainable business. The company nevertheless had enormous core strengths in its detailed knowledge of Asian manufacturing, its network of local offices, and its ability to move goods. At the same time, its largest product area, garments and textiles, was increasingly characterized by end users who did not want to own manufacturing facilities and who were ineffective at grappling with the rapidly shifting Asian manufacturing landscape. Victor and William seized the opportunity by approaching apparel designers like Levi Strauss and Abercrombie & Fitch with an offer to improve their choice of outsourcers and the management of those outsourcers. Over time, customer by customer, value-chain step by step, Li & Fung moved into adjacencies that have made the company into a highly sophisticated business that can now manage the complete supply chain, from raw material selection and negotiation to delivery of finished garments to Western distribution centers.

Information technology has further enabled the management, tracking, and measurement of such a disparate network—and demonstrated real efficiencies and cost savings to customers. As a result, Li & Fung has experienced a surge in revenues from 13.3 billion HK$ in 1997 to 33 billion HK$ in 2001, with a return on equity of more than 35 percent. In discussing his strategy of value chain and customer adjacency expansion, Victor Fung emphasizes the company's decision to organize around its customers. In fact, some business units are dedicated entirely to a single customer, a structure that creates clear accountability as well as an ability to clone itself and nurture major new customers. Li & Fung has now attained the scale that allows it to achieve a goal that Victor describes as having 30 to 70 percent of the capacity of its major suppliers. In 1995, Li & Fung purchased Inchcape Buying Services, its largest competitor, to provide a way to extend its network further, into adjacent regions like India and other product areas. The story of Li & Fung illustrates how movement into successive adjacencies (steps of the value chain, supply-chain management services, information services) can redefine the economics of a stagnating business and create the opportunity to maintain growth for some time to come.

Lloyds: Revitalizing the Core Through Adjacencies

Lloyds Bank traces its origin back to 1765, when John Taylor and Sampson Lloyd set up a private banking business in Birmingham, England. More than two hundred years later, in the early 1980s, Lloyds was one of the Big Four commercial banks in the United Kingdom, with branch operations extending from California to Korea. But it was not performing well; the *Times* referred to its black horse symbol as "quite literally, the dark horse of the high street, placed well down the field behind the other Big Four banks."[7] In 1983, the company had a return on equity of 12 percent, well below its cost of capital, a price-to-earnings ratio (P/E ratio) of only 7 in the stock market, and low growth. By 2000, the situation had reversed. Lloyds was arguably one of the best-performing financial services companies in the world. It had doubled shareholder value every three years over the seventeen years between 1983 and 2000 and had achieved return on equity of over 30 percent. Earnings had grown rapidly and the company enjoyed a Triple A rating. One of the key factors in this turnaround was the leadership of Sir Brian

Pitman, who became chief executive in 1983 and retired as chairman early in 2001.

Adjacencies played a major part in this turnaround in three ways. First, Pitman exited from previous expansions that showed no prospects of paying off, moves ranging from withdrawing from California to selling off Grindlay's Bank. Second, he acted decisively to avoid a potential disaster. Lloyds elected to be the only one of the Big Four not to enter the investment banking business during the "Big Bang" period of banking deregulation in 1986. Pitman elaborates:

> Our people said, "We'll have to get into this investment banking business now. Barclay is doing it, NatWest is doing it, the Americans will do it. If we don't, we will lose our corporate customers." Some on the board said this was the biggest opportunity ever, the Big Bang. I remained unconvinced. I did not see how we could compete effectively and be different.
>
> So, after these decisions, we got on with the more mundane business of building the best retail bank in the country while others were fighting about how to pay investment bankers, how to go after this bit of business, how to spend all that money. We had not withdrawn from the fastest-growing and biggest U.K. market opportunity, namely, the market for retail financial services.[8]

Instead, Lloyds took another look at its network of two thousand branches, viewing it as a retail distribution network, not merely a collection of relatively autonomous local units. The first new product adjacency was mortgages, through the purchase of Cheltenham & Gloucester, the leading mortgage company. The resulting "store within a store" was a huge success, says Pitman. "At the peak, over 50 percent of their sales went through our branches. The branch managers loved this arrangement since it was the best product in the country. We got the return on equity in the branch network up to 35 percent after tax as a result of this product move." From here, he explains, a natural extension was to begin selling insurance:

> We saw ourselves more and more as a distribution company.
> The cost of acquiring customers was low, and the extra mar-
> gin return was high. So many people make decisions when
> they take out a mortgage. They have never had to think about
> mortgage protection, about life assurance, about insuring
> things in the house, about insuring the house. I think it is
> perfectly possible to go on for a long time with this idea. We
> began to introduce all sorts of value-added services.

Another application of this adjacency expansion strategy into
product lines was to purchase other bank networks and apply their
expanded product strategy. Pitman says that this was the approach
taken by Lloyds in acquiring Trustee Savings Bank (TSB) with its
one thousand branches: "We could then transfer some of their ideas
and some of our ideas into the enlarged network. Cross-selling increased substantially and there is still a long way to go."

Few companies have risen from mediocrity to superiority
through strategy hinging so critically on a series of adjacency decisions. As I argue throughout this book, the management team that
applies rigor, not a vague sense of creativity or gut instinct, wins the
long-term adjacency game. Lloyds did just that.

The companies profiled briefly here—STMicroelectronics, UPS,
Li & Fung, and Lloyds TSB—enjoy uncommonly high success rates
in moving into adjacencies surrounding their cores. All have fundamentally strong core assets on which to build, relatively conservative
and rigorous approaches to selecting adjacencies, and noteworthy
attention to detail in execution. But what is the case of more typical
companies? What drives their odds? Is it better for them to focus on
increasing the odds of success or reducing the costs of failure?

Playing the Odds

One of the most profound developments in human health was the
creation of actuarial data on human mortality and morbidity. An

understanding of the risk factors for death and disease contributes greatly to society, from helping institutions decide where to focus research funding, to helping individuals choose their own diets. The first actuarial tables, developed in 1747 by James Hodgson, were unsophisticated. Only a full century later did actuaries accumulate and assimilate the detailed information that, for instance, established the link between the incidence of infectious disease in Victorian England and poor sanitation, especially the presence of rats. Since then, researchers have developed increasingly sophisticated statistics, from the risk of driving without a seat belt to the odds of contracting an illness from eating sushi. Such statistics shape our view of the world and the choices we make.

Though wealth is created on our planet primarily through business, there is no source, no actuarial equivalent, to address many basic questions regarding risk. Just try to find answers to relatively straightforward questions like: How often do distant followers in a business transform and attain sustainable economics? What are the odds of achieving a successful business turnaround? How often do large mergers actually create value? And so on.

In looking at adjacency expansion moves, my research team and I combed the literature, and we conducted our own independent analysis to understand as completely as possible the odds that major growth initiatives would truly drive a new source of sustained, profitable growth. We found, in our own data as well as in the secondary data, the success rate to be only about one in four. *Just 25 percent of investments in growth initiatives, most of them true adjacency expansions, created value and added to growth.*

Of 160 reports worldwide we were able to find on the topic of growth, only twenty-four contain sufficient sample size and make clear assumptions regarding the criteria of success. The average success rate for new products is about 30 percent; for start-ups, below 10 percent; for joint ventures, about 20 percent; and for related acquisitions, about 30 percent. These studies span a wide range of methods and quality of data, but all show how hard it is to find and execute on new sources of growth in a company.

In addition to this search of the literature, we conducted two further fact-finding initiatives. One was a worldwide survey of 138 executives conducted jointly by Bain & Company and the Economist Intelligence Unit. We asked these executives to estimate the percentage of their companies' initiatives to move into new adjacencies that they felt were truly successful. Their estimate in aggregate was only 25 percent. Across individuals, however, the experience varied widely—as it does in the CEO interviews and case studies featured in this book—from zero to more than 80 percent.

The second initiative was to build a database of 181 adjacency moves of major U.S. and U.K. public companies, randomly selected, from 1995 to 1997 (recent enough to have data, but before the Internet era of more reckless investing). We then researched the results through press releases, analyst reports, press coverage, and sometimes direct contact with the company. These adjacency moves spanned the full range of approaches, from new businesses (25) to movement up or down the value chain (21) to new channels (15) to new customer segments (36) to geographic expansion (30) to major new product launches (54). We found that these six categories accounted for virtually all types of single-move adjacencies. Across this sample, only 27 percent of adjacency moves could be considered successful. About 25 percent were clear failures, with the others having neutral or ambiguous returns.

It is not impossible to determine exactly how much of the wide variation in experiences across companies is a function of the strength of the core business, of sheer luck, of superior ability to select adjacencies, or of execution. After several years of work on adjacency expansion, however, I believe that the variation is due more to the position of the core business and the skill of management than to luck.

For example, one study found that frequent acquirers of other companies became more skilled at doing deals and integrating the acquisitions over time, thereby increasing their odds of success relative to competitors. Witness the extraordinary growth of GE Capital through more than 170 acquisitions from 1990 to

2000, during which the business essentially became an acquisition machine.

Analysis of the success rates of major product launches reveals that if a company is a dominant leader in its category, it is three times more likely than a follower to achieve success. Procter & Gamble has tracked its own success and failure rates and assesses the failure rate in the industry at about 85 to 90 percent. That is, of all the new products introduced or tested in the market, only 10 to 15 percent are actively on the shelf, still being sold, two years later. Procter & Gamble's target is to minimize the cost of failure by conducting extensive premarket testing and being willing to shift gears and invest massively in those products that satisfy the company's rigorous criteria for test success and market potential. As A. G. Lafley, CEO of P&G, says, "Homo sapiens are incredibly complex and impossible to predict. You have to have a repeatable system for getting ideas, exposing them to consumers, for test marketing, for measuring response. We at P&G test market more than anyone else because the failure rate in the industry is so high and the consumer is so unpredictable."[9]

As Lafley so clearly puts it, the unpredictability of the market can taint every adjacency move. Most of this book consequently focuses on the controllable dimensions of adjacency expansion moves that can either lower the cost of failure or increase the odds of success.

The Pressures for Adjacency Moves

A somewhat surprising finding in this study of the search for profitable growth is the extent to which pressure to make adjacency moves exists across the gamut of business situations. It is felt by strong leaders, gushing cash, with opportunities hurtling at them from all directions, as well as by companies whose industries are in decline, or are falling hopelessly far behind competitively, and who wonder if they should make one final shot to leap to a new lily pad.

Strong leaders in robust markets epitomize the epithet of Sun Tzu: "The more opportunities I seize, the more opportunities multiply before me." Strong core market growth can actually heighten anxiety about finding future sources of profitable growth to maintain such exceptional momentum. As the U.S. expansion program for The Home Depot approaches saturation, where does the company go? It has tried smaller formats, forays into services and installation, and even new retail concepts, with limited success. Will it take a major adjacency move to reignite growth, or does the current core still hold untapped growth prospects? As Dell, a $35 billion company with a $3.5 billion cash flow, looks at growth beyond the PC, it has begun a range of adjacency initiatives, including low-end switches, printers, and supplies; handheld devices; and even retail kiosks—and these are but a handful of the hundreds of choices that a company in Dell's commanding position has before it. But which to choose? How many? At what rate? How to maintain the remarkable momentum of the past?

Strong leaders in weak core markets face a different dilemma. Organic expansion plus "close-in" adjacency moves (like the Dell example) might not be enough to satisfy their investors' aspirations—or their own. Hillenbrand Industries provides a classic example of this situation. Hillenbrand is in two businesses—mechanical hospital beds and caskets. Both markets are growing at less than 5 percent per year, and Hillenbrand has more than a 70 percent market share in each. Room to grow share is limited, as is the potential to grow the market (driven by hospital use and burials). As a result, Hillenbrand is forced to examine adjacencies that utilize its basic skills but that might be several steps away from its historic cores.

Another version of the Hillenbrand situation is the company with a strong niche position within a larger market. The company may feel that it needs to grow, but recognizes that, with insufficient growth opportunities in its historic subspecialty, it must venture out into the broader arena. One example of a company facing this situation is Enterprise Rent-A-Car, which has a commanding market share of replacement rentals from body shops and insurance companies but encounters entrenched competitors in every adjacent direction of business rentals (Hertz and Avis), leisure rentals (Alamo), fleet leasing (PHH and GE Capital), and so on. Truly one company's adjacency is another company's core, in a market with many related customer and product segments such as vehicle rental.

Paradoxically, leadership businesses have the most to lose in adjacency expansions. Their valuable core franchises would be put at risk by major forays into the wrong adjacency or by premature abandonment of the core as an investment vehicle. And this risk is compounded by the abundance of temptation: The strongest businesses with cash to invest have opportunities brought to them every day by a long line of investment banks and deal makers. During discussions of adjacency expansion, Sir Christopher Gent, CEO of Vodafone, remarked that CEOs should be judged by the opportunities that they decline as well as those they accept. Adjacency expansion for a strong leader is reminiscent of Napoleon's famous statement "The most dangerous moment comes with victory."

At the other end of the spectrum are businesses in weak competitive positions or collapsing core markets and whose management would like nothing better than to jump to a better position, even a different business. However, the data show that few weak followers—in fact, only about 5 percent—materially change their positions over time. The more typical example is Budget Rent a Car, once the number six car rental company in the United States. The business has had five different owners since 1986 and five different strategies. Some strategies have employed adjacency moves such as entering the travel business (a failure) or purchasing the Ryder truck rental business (number two to U-Haul). But salvation was not to be found. In 2001, Budget lost $597 million on sales of $2.2 billion. In 2002, the company declared bankruptcy and was purchased at a fire sale by Cendant to be absorbed into that company's Avis business. Nonetheless, it is hard not to sympathize with managers who run these businesses and feel a sense of frustration bordering on desperation.

Another situation in which adjacency expansion is on the minds of management teams is when an industry is in turbulence. During the 1970s, only about 10 to 15 percent of industries were encountering major shifts in the basis of competition. During the 1990s, the number was approaching 50 percent, with tremendous turbulence in major industrial sectors, from financial services to publishing to airlines to many retail sectors.

Turbulence can take a variety of forms. One form is when an entire sector that has been protected from the full pressure of competition suddenly has its protective shield removed. An example is the deregulation of public utilities in the United States in the 1990s, when company after company rushed into adjacencies ranging from telecommunications to global expansion to financial hedging. A second form of turbulence is the rare, but stressful, situation of the *melting core*. A core melts down when the industry or market itself is in rapid structural decline. What happened to the typewriter industry with the advent of word processors is an example. The magnetic tape industry's giving way to optical storage is another, and the photographic film industry's encounter with digital imaging is a third. In each of these situations, companies like Imation (in storage) or Polaroid and Kodak (in photography) have faced strong pressure to find adjacent moves to serve as stepping-stones to a more stable future.

Each of these business situations—from strong leadership to followership, from growing market to melting core—has its own internal and external pressures to push out from the boundaries of its core business into adjacent areas. Chapter 4 will discuss the odds and formulas for success under these different conditions. The exception is, of course, the company with leadership in a stable or growing market. We estimate that only 12 percent of businesses start with this set of fortunate circumstances as their platform in the search for sustained, profitable growth. Most companies—nearly 90 percent of them—exist in much-less-than-ideal conditions.

The Vocabulary of Adjacency Expansion

Throughout this book, I will use a relatively simple set of constructs to describe the various types of adjacency moves and their attributes. There are essentially six primary ways, or vectors, along which the boundaries of a business can be pushed out (figure 1-2). In a sense, these extremely basic ways of shifting along a single dimension are like atoms of growth that can be combined into much more complex molecules that constitute most strategies that we see.

1. *Product adjacencies:* Selling a new product or new services to core customers is one of the most commonly pursued and highest-potential adjacencies. The creation of IBM Global Services for IBM's hardware customers illustrates one of the most successful growth strategies triggered by a product adjacency. Global Services now constitutes 40 percent of the company.

2. *Geographic adjacencies:* Moving into a new geographic area is a type of adjacency move that companies consistently underestimate in complexity, hence the lower-than-average success rate. An example is Vodafone's expansion from the United Kingdom into Europe, into the United States through the AirTouch merger, into Germany through the purchase of Mannesmann, and into Japan through the acquisition of a majority share in Japan Telecom and its J-Phone subsidiary.

3. *Value chain adjacencies:* Going up or down the value chain into an entirely new set of activities is one of the most difficult forms of adjacency expansion. Merck's acquisition and recent divestiture of Medco, a mail-order drug distributor, illustrates a value chain adjacency. Another example is the entrance of LVMH, the luxury goods company that owns twenty-five fashion brands, from Fendi to Louis Vuitton, into the retail business by the purchase of Sephora and Duty

FIGURE 1-2

Many Types of Adjacencies Can Radiate from the Core

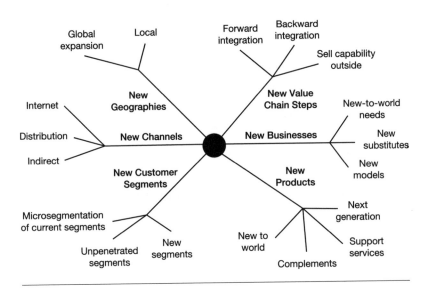

Free Shoppers in 1996. At the time, LVMH announced that these purchases were complementary to its activities. In 2001, the company changed its point of view and announced that these units would be divested, indicating that this retail segment was found to be "noncore."

4. *Channel adjacencies:* If successful, the move into a new channel can produce an enormous source of new value. If not, it can turn into a true Waterloo. For example, EAS (Experimental and Applied Science), the leading sports-supplement company, has had great success in making minor changes in the formulation, packaging, and celebrity sponsorship of its Myoplex sports bars, originally sold in specialty nutrition stores, and quickly becoming a leader in its category selling to Wal-Mart. By contrast, the entry of Dell into the mass retail channel with personal computers caused massive disruption in pricing, factory processes,

marketing, and sales and led to the only time in which Dell lost money—1993, when it lost $36 million. In June 1994, Dell made the courageous decision to exit the indirect retail channel even though at the time it was building a large warehouse to serve Wal-Mart. This exit move allowed Dell to resume its trajectory to become the best-performing company in the United States during the 1990s.

5. *Customer adjacencies:* Modifying a proven product or technology to enter a totally new customer segment is a major adjacency move for many companies. Examples include the creation of Kids "R" Us by Toys "R" Us, the move by Staples from retail into the delivery of office products to small businesses, and Charles Schwab's expansion of advisory services to target high-net-worth individuals.

6. *New business adjacencies:* Building a new business around a strong capability, essentially repurposing it, is the rarest form of adjacency move—and the most difficult to pull off. The classic example is when American Airlines created the Sabre reservation system, which grew into a spin-off now worth more than the airline itself. Sabre, in turn, went on to create a new business adjacency of its own in Travelocity.

These singular moves, like atoms connecting to form molecules, can be combined into a series of interlocking moves. Sometimes there is an opportunity to make a series of similar single-adjacency moves, like Vodafone's serial acquisitions of local providers to build a global wireless network. Other times, there is an opportunity to create a sequence of moves of various types that truly redefine the core business. The sequence of moves that Victor Fung choreographed to turn Li & Fung from a trading company into a supply-chain management company combined customer, value chain, geographic, and even channel moves.

The chapters of this book are organized around the steps of a thought process that companies might adopt as they consider their growth strategies and adjacency moves (figure 1-3). We begin in

FIGURE 1 - 3

Map of the Book

Visualizing the ideal	Evaluating adjacency moves	Balancing adjacency moves with the core	Executing adjacency moves	Transforming the core through adjacencies

chapter 2 with the idea of visualizing the ideal adjacency moves, focusing on the characteristic of repeatability to drive wave after wave of growth over time, constantly refining and adapting the process, moving down a learning curve, and building up competitive advantage. Such repeatability is at the heart of some of the great cases of sustained, profitable growth, ranging from Dell to STMicroelectronics to Vodafone to Li & Fung. Defining the right criteria and the right process to make the decision to invest in an adjacency, or an entire vector of adjacency moves, can be a critical and defining moment for a company. Many of the interviewed CEOs described how important this step is and how often they believe it is done in a way not sufficiently clear or rigorous. Chapter 3 looks at twenty-four companies in carefully matched pairs to identify and compare the handful of most critical criteria that needs to be considered in any world-class decision process regarding growth investments.

Building growth on a core business that is prepared to support it, and for which the new adjacency moves might even reinforce the strength of the core, rather than draining it of energy, is critical. This issue of timing and of assessing the state of the core to support growth is examined in chapter 4. The CEOs who helped shape the materials and examples for this book emphasized over and over a handful of issues related to the execution of adjacency moves in the context of an organization that is, by its nature, built around and obsessed about the core. Four areas were central to the success of these companies and to the comments of the CEOs. These areas are examined in chapter 5. Finally, chapter 6 looks at how adjacency expansions done rapidly and effectively provide the best method to transform a company and redefine its core business.

The Promise of This Book

Pushing out the boundaries of a core business is one of the most difficult management challenges. The typical odds of success are low. Managers have a built-in bias to underestimate and underprepare for the ultimate complexity of these moves. Stock price swings and volatility are driven strongly by perceptions about adjacency expansion. And a large proportion of CEO departures occurs in the presence of adjacency expansions gone wrong. Yet, in spite of these risks and penalties, the movement into adjacencies is the way that businesses ultimately find their next wave of profitable growth, without which they eventually stagnate and may even decline.

In my interviews of CEOs for this book, I started by asking what they believed were the key events in the development, shaping, and growth trajectory of their company. Invariably, the CEOs listed key adjacency moves as among the most defining events. Andy Taylor of Enterprise Rent-A-Car pointed to the decision to move from leasing cars into renting cars to dealerships, which triggered the business Enterprise has today. Tom Stemberg of Staples talked about the movement from retail stores into distribution to small businesses, which spurred a sequence of adjacency moves that re-shaped the company. Helmut Kormann of the leading paper machine company, Voith, cited several specific moves going back more than one hundred years. These adjacency moves, ranging from the entry into the paper machine fabrics business to a recent entry into on-site services, led to and reinforced the company's growth trajectory and leadership position today. Bob Norton of FTD emphasized how critical it was to make an adjacency move with the introduction of FTD.com, which allowed the company to link directly to customers to supplement its network of links between florists and defend the core against new competitors. These types of difficult, sometimes even agonizing growth moves punctuated the historical timelines in the minds of each CEO.

If there is one thing I have gained from this voyage through the growth moves of so many companies in so wide a range of situations, it is an appreciation for the depth of the challenge and an unshakable belief that there is never a silver-bullet solution. Rather, the promise of growth lies in methods that allow you to decide correctly, to tilt the odds in your favor, and to control the cost of failures when they inevitably occur. The hope of this book is that the examples, data, and frameworks analyzed here can help managers make and manage adjacency decisions better.

Visualizing the Ideal

The First Principle of Adjacency Growth

Repeatability is the essence of mastery and control. "Relentless repeatability" was a phrase used by golf legend Ben Hogan to describe the driving force behind his professional success, and it is an apt term for one of the most critical elements in the growth of companies, the discovery of a repeatable formula to drive profitable growth. Hogan, the human embodiment of this concept, was known for playing golf with "the burning frigidity of dry ice," and a repeatability that remains legendary. But, as with adjacency expansion, this repeatability did not come easily. It required intense preparation and attention to surprising levels of detail, and in so doing, Hogan distanced himself from his competitors for a decade.

For instance, Hogan was known to spend more time on the practice tee than any other professional did, often remaining until his hands would bleed. Fellow golfers avoided adjoining hotel rooms because Hogan would practice in the evening, chipping against the wall or into a chair and creating a consistent thump, thump, thump into the night. His attention to repeatability even went as far as choice of golf balls. Hogan would take crates of golf balls to his room, float them in the bath (they floated more then), and see which balls always turned in the same direction downward, signaling asymmetry of the inner elastic winding. He would then discard these imperfect spheres in favor of perfectly repeating golf balls. Mastery and control through repetition.

Mastery at the customer level and control over competitive dynamics are the keys to earning profits in business. Focused companies that have a strong, or dominant, core and that hit on a repeatable formula for extending their strength to new arenas are the breeder reactors of business. These companies create value year after year, while the majority of businesses live in a twilight of uncertainty, feeling more controlled by outside forces than by their own will.

It is the companies that skip from topic to topic, hunting and pecking like an unskilled typist, looking for the next adjacency, which is only loosely tied to the skills of the last one, that never achieve a real breakout. If I were to characterize my search for the perfect business adjacency through our mass of case studies and interviews, relentless, focused repeatability would be at the top of the list. About two-thirds of the most successful, sustained-growth companies studied in depth for this book have one or two powerful, repeatable formulas, "adjacency machines" that generate waves of new growth over time. Yet, it is a dimension not often brought up in many business meetings about profitable growth, because the managers are often focusing on the "next big move."

This chapter will make the case for the hidden powers of repeatability in business strategies and suggest how management teams can use this insight.

Olam: High Growth from Repeatability in Low-Growth Markets

The story of Olam shows how a repeatable formula for adjacency expansion can propel and shape a company from start-up in one country and one product to a large, successful, and complex business fourteen years later.

I first encountered Olam during a trip to Singapore, where I was on a panel discussing the search for growth for companies in Asia. To my right was a quiet, unassuming, Harvard-educated British citizen of Indian origin, Sunny Verhese, CEO of Olam, a global agricultural raw materials supplier. When it came time for Verhese to describe the history of the company and its sequence of moves into adjacencies, the room became transfixed. He told a remarkable story of his company and how it created a relentlessly repeatable approach to its business from a standing start in a range of unique, difficult, and developing markets. During the fourteen years since its inception, Olam has created a financially successful growth engine that has seen its revenues grow from zero in 1989 to $1.2 billion in 2003. Even in the last six years, the company has continued growing revenues at 28 percent and earnings at 31 percent, and has achieved an average return on capital of 35 percent. Remarkably, the entire growth has been organic and has taken place in an industry of agricultural raw materials that grows at roughly half the rate of world GDP, a mere 2 percent.

Today, Olam is a global leader in the supply of various agricultural raw materials such as cocoa, coffee, cashews, peanuts, sesame seeds, and shea nuts to large, global packaged-food multinationals such as Kraft, General Foods, Sara Lee, Nestlé, and Mars. The company provides a one-stop solution to its customers by being integrated across the entire supply chain, from the "farm gate" in the producing countries to the "factory gate" of its customers in the consuming markets. Supply-chain management consists of sourcing and origination, primary processing of raw materials into intermediate products, managing the inland and marine logistics/storage/transportation, and handling the trading, marketing, distribution, and risk management of these agricultural products. Most of the commodities that Olam has chosen to supply are grown in developing or emerging markets, while most of the consumption occurs in developed markets. For example, roughly 70 percent of world cocoa production, a key ingredient in chocolate manufacture, occurs in four West African countries—Côte d'Ivoire,

Ghana, Nigeria, and Cameroon—whereas most of the chocolate consumption takes place in the developed countries.

When Olam was first setting up its operations (late 1980s and early 1990s), most agricultural commodity trade in the producing countries was controlled by government commodity boards or state monopolies. These commodity boards had evolved into large bureaucracies, with opaque decision-making practices and in some cases rampant corruption. The result was that there were often significant leakages, with the farmer ultimately realizing a small fraction of the export value of the commodity (estimated at 33 percent of the export value). Most of these producing countries at that time were also facing considerable economic difficulties, which prompted them to seek assistance from the World Bank and the IMF. One of the reforms insisted upon by the IMF was for the restructuring of their commodity boards and state monopolies. These liberalization measures and the consequent transparency they have brought about have proved to be effective, with the farmer now appropriating a little over 70 percent of the export value of the commodity versus the previous 33 percent.

Olam was quick to recognize that these changes fundamentally altered the rules of the game in its industry. Olam stepped into the void by increasing its investment in procurement and logistics infrastructure in these producing countries. They pitched to their customers that rather than taking the significant Nigeria or Côte d'Ivoire risk directly, they had an opportunity to reduce risk by contracting with Olam.

Verhese states that Olam's global strategy is to build competitive advantage by "out-origining" his competitors and concurrently building marketing, trading, and risk management skills. The repeatability of multiproduct cross sourcing within a given geography has helped Olam develop a more favorable cost position compared to its competitors which are organized in individual product silos (cocoa, coffee, etc.) and therefore have not achieved the repeatability of Olam.

Cracking the code on the origin management challenges and being able to leverage this across similar emerging markets in Africa and Asia has created a unique competitive advantage for Olam that has become the core of the company. Recognizing this, Verhese has insisted that each of his managers, as an essential rite of passage, lives and works for a reasonable length of time in these producing countries. He himself lived in rural Nigeria for three and a half years to get firsthand experience of how the agricultural products supply chain worked.

The repeating sequence can be seen in cocoa. Olam started supplying cocoa from a single producing country, again Nigeria, to chocolate manufacturers and cocoa grinders. The same customers were also sourcing cocoa from other countries to create specific blends to produce chocolates of a unique flavor that underscored their brand identity. Understanding this, Olam expanded into other cocoa producing countries and is today present and sourcing from every key cocoa producing origin. Through its repeated adjacency moves, Olam has quickly become one of the top three global suppliers of cocoa beans and products.

In coffee, we see the same principles of expansion. Olam began supplying robusta coffees from India to various coffee roasters in Europe. Having developed a critical mass of roasters for its Indian coffee, the company rapidly moved into other robusta growing countries to service the varying needs of its original customer base. Today it is the world's largest supplier of robusta coffee from eleven producing countries. Olam has been able to establish this pattern of repeatability in thirty-five countries in which it has operations because it was changing only one variable at a time, in this case geography, built on a strong existing core position, and with customers at the other end providing a source of secure demand. The formula through Olam's history has consisted of sequences of one-step adjacency moves, this time just varying the commodity or product or geography. Country adjacencies have led to more requests to handle other agricultural commodities, while product adjacencies have led to new opportunities to source that product in new countries. On top of this repeated cycling between new products and new geographies emerged a third vector of value chain adjacencies to process existing products in existing countries. For example, the company moved from raw cashew nut trading to the shelling and blanching of raw cashew nuts into cashew kernels in India, Vietnam, and Brazil, the three key cashew processing centers in the world. Similarly, it backward integrated into the processing of cocoa beans into cocoa butter, cake, powder, and liquor; the crushing of shea nuts into shea butter; the grading and hulling of sesame seed; the hulling cleaning, grading, and color sorting of raw coffee into green coffee; the processing of green coffee into soluble coffee; the drying, grading, and sorting of peanuts; and the ginning of seed cotton into cotton lint. This sequence of adjacency moves is shown in figure 2-1. From one country and one product, Olam has grown into a presence in thirty-five countries and produces twelve products.

Olam has two rigorous sets of investment criteria applied to adjacent moves—one of which is financial (concurrently achieving revenue growth, profit growth, and returns above the cost of capital) and one involving its "rules of the game." These rules involve specific criteria related to origin and product market position (the company should be in the top three globally in that product and should be physically present in all the key producing countries), connectedness to the current core of products and countries, and strong end-market customer presence. Verhese says that Olam's repeatable adjacency formula can be projected forward, and "makes it pretty clear to us where our next $1 billion of revenue will come from."

As with all growing companies, some moves along the way did not work out. For example, Olam entered and then exited the market for black pepper and for rubber. Through these experiences, says Verhese, the company has continued to tighten and make more rigorous its investment criteria for adjacency moves: "The combination of customer need, shared cost, and shared capability has become the sweet spot for our adjacency expansion."[1]

FIGURE 2 - 1

Olam's Repeatable Formula of Adjacency Moves

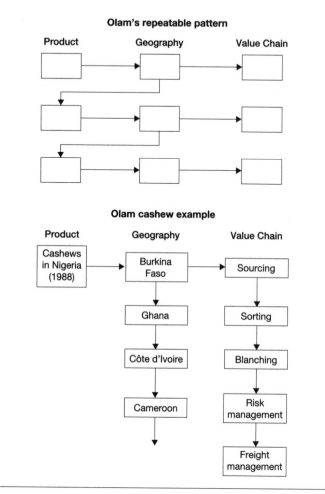

In the study in this book of companies that succeeded in adjacency expansion, there was a consistent theme of continuously tightening criteria by which investments are made as the company gained experience with what did and did not work. Given Olam's position of having wholly owned subsidiaries in thirty-five countries, seventeen of them in Africa, numerous tempting opportunities stream across the desk of the CEO. One proposal was an offer for the pan-African franchise for computer and software education in partnership with a leading publicly listed company in that field. While on the surface the proposal seemed financially attractive, Verhese decided against it: "After much internal debate, we passed on this opportunity, as we felt that this was at least a three- or four-step-removed adjacency and would detract from our continued investment in our core business, especially in terms of our attention and focus. We still had enough headroom to extract value from our core business that would keep us going for the next five years."

I have started with the story of Olam because, like the Ben Hogan analogy, it epitomizes the combination of mastery and control through repetition in one of the toughest businesses around.

Sources for Case Studies

The data for this chapter were drawn from case studies of one hundred companies, many including interviews with senior executives. Of these studies, we focused on twenty-five companies that had achieved sustainable growth performance far in excess of their peer group, that represented a mixture of industries, and that spanned a wide range of geographies. For each of these twenty-five, we conducted CEO interviews, prepared a full profile of the company's growth history, and, in some cases, interviewed other supporting senior management. The companies are listed in the appendix.

In total, these companies achieved an impressive record of profitable growth. From 1992 to 2002, they grew from $107 billion in revenues to $276 billion, outgrowing their respective industries by nearly threefold, on average. These twenty-five companies increased their earnings from $7 billion to $23 billion during that period and created over $500 billion of value in the stock market. This value has persisted despite the stock market collapse of recent years. On average, the companies returned 22 percent annually to shareholders. Adjacency expansions were an important part of their growth.

Three critical factors, potentially the most important three root causes of sustained and profitable growth, coexisted in at least eighteen of the twenty-five companies. If this entire book had to be boiled down to three elements, it would be these: First, each company had a strong core that constituted a stable and suitable launch-pad for a sequence of growth initiatives beyond the core. Second, these companies hit upon a repeatable formula for adjacency expansion that generated strong economic and competitive benefits in its repeated application. Third, these companies' formulas were, 80 percent of the time, built around specific and deep insights about customer behavior that could be replicated in different products or segments or circumstances with high odds of success and profit. Some examples would be Lloyds Bank's approach to turning its branch network into a broader distribution vehicle for insurance, mortgages, and related products for its core customer base, or Olam's oscillation between product segments and geographies. About 15 percent of the adjacency formulas were based on clear scale economics of production in the build-out of a network. Tesco (the most successful food retailer in Europe in the 1990s) in food, the build-out of the global UPS delivery system, and the expansion of Vodafone are prime examples here. Fewer than 5 percent of the cases of repeatable adjacency expansions were situations of unique business models, or capabilities, that could be applied over and over to new competitive arenas. In a much larger set of case examples, in which we looked for the existence of a repeatable formula among the highest-performance companies, we found that these proportions of adjacency types held broadly. As such, most of this chapter is heavily focused on the dominant types, customer-driven adjacencies.

How Relentless Repeatability Creates Competitive Barriers

Repeatability in detailed operational processes has been shown over and over, since the early work on the experience curve in airfoil production, to drive productivity improvements. Less effort and research have focused on the importance of repeatability in growing a business. Finding a repeatable method of moving into new adjacencies, one after the other, has several clear benefits, each of which contributes to competitive advantage.

- *Learning curve effects:* A repeatable model allows an organization to be built around it, creating an adjacency machine with its own processes that can move down a learning curve in repeated application. GE Capital and Vodafone built expertise in acquisition evaluation and deal making by virtue of their desire to be serial acquirers. Our research across seventeen hundred companies indicates that serial acquirers—that is, companies doing more than three small deals per year—achieved 25 percent higher returns than did companies making fewer, but larger, acquisitions. One reason: the ability to build a focused organization around a repeated activity.

- *Reduced complexity:* In our discussions of P&G's ability to consistently outgrow its industry, A. G. Lafley emphasized that "complexity is the bane of a large organization. It strangles growth. It strangles everything."[2] We built a simulation model to look at how many adjacencies a company would have to attack successfully to outgrow a 3 percent growth market. The answer is that over five years, to achieve 6 percent growth using reasonable size and success rate assumptions, the company would have to attack fifteen adjacencies and achieve lasting success (and the organizational consequences) in seven of them. To achieve 9 percent growth, the figure rises to thirty-five growth moves and fourteen successes in five years—a tall order. Arguably, this excessive complexity is how Enron, which we calculate moved into thirty-four adjacencies over its last four years, got into trouble so quickly and so deeply. Repeatability allows fewer organizational variations.

- *Speed:* Speed is essential to growth. Doubling the speed at which an adjacency succeeds has a material impact on the growth rate of a business that is constantly attacking new areas surrounding its core. For example, consider a company in a 3 percent growth market that attacks two adjacent areas per year with a 40 percent success rate and a size potential of 5 percent of its total business. Our estimates show that if this company achieved most of its potential in two years instead of five, it would have a sustainable growth rate of more than 5 percent. The difference in growth rates creates a large difference in value over time. Repeatability dramatically lowers cycle time relative to the practice of shifting gears from one area to another.

- *Strategic clarity:* Clarity of communication about the growth strategy affects investor and employer confidence. Recall how the perception of value of future growth beyond the core affected stock prices (see chapter 1). The ability to describe a repeatable approach, constantly adapted to a range of new conditions, as shown in the Olam example, has a powerful influence on investors and employees. One survey of employees showed that one of the top two drivers of employee loyalty was the ability to understand and believe in the company's strategy for the future. Certainly, STMicroelectronics exists in one of the most complex markets. Yet, its CEO, Pasquale Pistorio, has repeatedly emphasized strategic clarity: "The strategy has stayed the same for many years, just applied and adapted in different ways. You can manage our strategy with just four guidelines. I now believe that any good strategy must fit on a single page, emphasize the clear competitive advantages, and show how that can be used over and over again."[3]

- *Ability to "drill down":* For many businesses, the key to growth comes from a *drilling down,* that is, an understanding of the details of the business and the execution of them. The difficulty that well-funded competitors have in catching up to companies with a well-oiled, repeatable formula is, in part, due to the challenge of catching up in these details. Whether it is the multitude of coffee start-ups trying to replicate

Starbucks—a concept that looks easy on the surface, but is devilish to get right in the details—or Compaq's unsuccessful attempts to copy Dell's direct model, getting the details right is not an easy task. This chapter later examines how some companies have developed analytical techniques that can be applied repeatedly to find new growth insights from drilling down into the customers' needs in greater detail.

These benefits (learning curve effects, reduced complexity, speed, strategic clarity, and the ability to drill down on details) are the hallmarks of companies that are the most successful at expanding themselves through a repeatable method. Repeatability can create a sizable competitive barrier. At several points in this book, I will use a simple simulation model to study the effect of adjacency performance on growth rates and value creation. Measures of performance include the rate of launching new initiatives, their potential size, the ramp-up rate, the success rate, and the cost of failure.

Small improvements in performance along these dimensions can increase the overall growth rate of a business considerably. If a company in a 3 percent growth market achieved the potential from its adjacency moves 30 percent faster, handled three—not two—adjacency initiatives per year, and had a success rate (through selection and implementation) of 60 percent instead of 30 percent, then the company would nearly double its growth rate, to 7.1 percent from 3.9 percent. Compounded over five years at a constant margin and P/E ratio, these differences in growth rate lead to a 50 percent difference in value creation by the end of the period. If the higher growth rate and repeatability leads also to a much higher P/E, as it inevitably would, the difference could be much larger. Our work on the math of growth and comparative success rates of similar companies shows over and over that management teams that focus primarily on finding few "big moves" are usually missing the point unless they have no alternative or are in the rare industry in the midst of unique structural changes that demand rapid, radical repositioning. These apparently small differences accumulate and are further magnified by stock market valuation habits to constitute a massive difference that could accrue from successful repeatability versus moderately successful "hunt and peck" growth.

Nike: An Adjacency Athlete

A remarkable study in contrasts of repeatability versus nonrepeatability is the story of the competitive battle of Nike and Reebok. In 1990, the two companies had uncannily identical financials. Nike's revenues were $2.3 billion; Reebok's were $2.2 billion. Nike's operating income was $481 million to Reebok's $300 million. Both companies were almost entirely focused on athletic shoes, with Nike focused more on performance athletes, while Reebok's focus was somewhat more diffuse. Both had well-known brands. By the end of a ten-year period, the companies' fortunes were quite different. Nike's market capitalization had increased by 380 percent while Reebok's had shrunk in half. Nike had a clear strategy apparent to all constituencies, consisting of a repeatable method it had developed and refined over the decade to attack one sport after another. Reebok's path was a mystery to those covering the company.

For example, Reebok had made unrelated investments, such as its purchase of the Boston Whaler boat company, at the same time that its core shoe business was under severe attack. The company moved from adjacency to adjacency without a clear commitment to any vector. Though Reebok referred to itself as a "sports and performance company, not a fashion and fitness company," some of its brand additions, such as Ralph Lauren and Polo Footwear, seemed inconsistent with that definition. In addition, the company had a series of troubled "me too" growth initiatives ranging from the "Shaq Attack" sneaker to the women's "Incubus" running shoe. The latter caused much consternation in 1997, when it was revealed that an incubus is a medieval spirit with bad intentions that lives to have sex with sleeping women.

While Reebok was dabbling in a variety of these unrelated ventures, Nike was recognizing its emerging repeatable formula. Like many companies, Nike took years to develop and hone its strategy, and even to realize the potential of its approach, which started with running in 1963. It moved to basketball with Michael Jordan's 1985 endorsement, moved into tennis in 1986 with John McEnroe as spokesperson, and then entered the 1990s picking up speed and moving into baseball, football, cycling, volleyball, hiking, soccer, and now golf.

Nike's recent entry into golf—one of the most demanding segments for marketing new products, with many entrenched, niche competitors—epitomizes the company's powerful formula. The company began by entering the market for golf shoes in 1988 against such niche competitors as Footjoy, selling primarily through sporting goods shops, not golf course professionals. In 1996, Nike signed a $100 million deal with Tiger Woods and launched heavily into golf apparel, including a signature TW line, and accessories like bags, eyewear, and gloves. Three years later, Nike entered a much more difficult market, golf balls, and Tiger Woods sent ripples through the golf community by switching from the leader, Titleist, to Nike for his own use. Almost instantly, Nike's share of golf balls bounced up to more than 6 percent in a crowded, competitive field. As the product line expanded, Nike signed more and more tour professionals to its roster and used massive advertising to disseminate the results of their wins. In an amazing three-year stretch at the British Open, Nike was able to announce in 1999 that Paul Lawrie had won the tournament using Nike golf shoes; in 2000 that Tiger Woods had won using the new golf balls; in 2001 that David Duval had won his first major tournament using the first line of Nike golf clubs.

The jury is out on whether the foray into the highly specialized, niche-filled market of golf will be completely successful. However, the power of a repeatable franchise is evident here (especially in comparison with the identically sized Reebok a decade earlier). The sequence is to move from shoes to apparel to hard goods, from soft entry to endorsement by leading athletes, and from U.S. entry to global distribution (figure 2-2). The power of the brand and athletes' endorsements of performance is hard for competitors to match. How do you compete when every U.S. track and field medalist in the Barcelona 1992 Olympics wears Nike apparel, or when Michael Jordan wears Nike shoes hitting the winning shot for the NBA championship, or when Tiger Woods wins his first golf

FIGURE 2 - 2

Nike's Repeatable Formula of Adjacency Moves

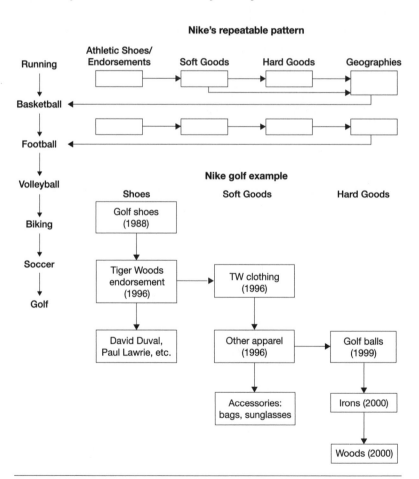

tournament by a personal best of twenty-five under par after switching to Nike's new irons? Nike has accomplished the implementation of this expansion formula without losing focus on its core shoe business, where it has increased global market share from 22 percent in 1990 to 38 percent in 2002, four times the share of its nearest competitor. This is the essence of strategic focus: increasing strength in the core while driving that market power into new adjacencies through a repeatable and adaptable set of methods.

So, what is in this story for the typical company? This example illustrates several key findings of this study of adjacency expansion. First, Nike took a while to find the pattern; it was not endowed with it at birth. Second, Nike's formula allowed it to pull away competitively from companies in the same arena that were watching its success, but unable to replicate it. Indeed, it was precisely the ability of Nike to replicate success that created expertise, an adjacency machine built around the concept, and that lured competitors to try to play Nike's game, unsuccessfully. Third, the formula is based on mining deeper and deeper insight about customer behavior. It is fundamentally focused on detailed customer usage patterns across an entire field of behavior and in a particular sport. Customer centricity is a characteristic of the vast majority of growth patterns and is the place to start. Finally, the formula has many elements to it. On its own, each element is less than one step from the core, but in total, the elements create a new business with elements that are a step or two away from the original core and create enormous competitive advantage in the process.

The Myth of the Perfect Company

A danger in business research on the "best performers" is that the conclusions simply do not apply universally. Certainly, the average artist will benefit from a study of Rembrandt; the average guitarist from a study of Segovia; the average writer from a study of Hemingway. However, the most rapid progress will also involve techniques accessible to those who have not yet achieved immortality. A surprising and consistent insight from all the case studies and interviews is how many of these companies had experienced past periods of slow growth, or even crisis, and which companies used techniques of strengthening and redefining their core business and, after that, adjacency expansion to change their direction.

Twenty of the twenty-five companies screened and profiled here experienced periods of financial crisis, stagnation, or near collapse and then recovered, stronger than ever. This finding was a surprise, noticed after the companies had been screened by performance and the interviews conducted. For many, this resurgence was fueled by a repeatable adjacency formula that they discovered, rediscovered or refined, and perfected. Li & Fung had experienced a total stoppage of growth and, over time, margin erosion from 15 percent to below 5 percent over a generation. Today, Li & Fung is ending a decade as one of the best-performing Asian companies. STMicroelectronics was formed from a subscale business owned by the Italian government in the mid-1980s and, under Pasquale Pistorio and his team, rose from a $100 million revenue level and a loss of nearly half that to a highly profitable company and one of the largest microprocessor fabricators and designers in the world. Lloyds TSB was at the bottom of the ranking of U.K. banks in the late 1970s. During the management of Sir Brian Pitman, the company found a repeatable formula, avoided some disastrous adjacency temptations, and rose to be one of the top-performing banks in the world.

Biogen was on the brink of bankruptcy in 1988 when Jim Vincent took over as CEO: "In my first year, we reduced the size of the company by over 50 percent, cutting from 450 to 220 people. We shut down 85 percent of the research programs. We went back to the drawing board on our strategy, and we found in the dustbin the hepatitis science patent position. This provided the economic base of $200 million per year to fill the gap until we could build a company to get our own drugs to market."[4]

Perhaps the most dramatic example of a company that had a near-death experience but rallied through a repeatable formula is Dell. From its successful IPO in 1988 to 1992, the company grew from $150 million to $2 billion in sales; earnings grew even faster, from $9.4 million to $102 million. Then, in 1993, Dell made a number of strategic adjacency moves, particularly its foray into the retail business—a move that stopped the company's trajectory in its tracks. That same year, Dell's earnings plummeted to a loss of $36 million, even though the company grew by 44 percent (in part because of retail). The company suddenly found itself in the throes of severe self-doubt about the full potential of its direct-to-customer model for selling personal computers. Dell, unlike many companies in such a crisis, made all the right moves. For the period 1990 to 2000, Dell was named the company of the decade. The company attained revenues of $32 billion, earnings of $2.3 billion, and an astounding 355 percent return on invested capital.

As these examples show, few successful companies emerge from the egg perfectly formed, with a clear winning and repeatable formula in hand. If a company fears that its best days are over, these examples should give it cause to be more optimistic.

Mining Customer Insights for Repeatability

The Nike and Olam stories illustrate different ways to look at a customer group in the search for profitable growth. Throughout the CEO interviews we conducted, we constantly heard the refrain that not only does it all start with the customer, but also that the CEOs were constantly finding that their organizations did not really understand the customer's needs, behaviors, frustrations, categories, and situations as well as the CEO thought they should. Furthermore, every time they invested the resources to get closer to the customer (through some of the techniques described below), they often found new sources of growth—sometimes organic growth in the core, occasionally a new vector of adjacency growth, and, sometimes, even the basis of a repeatable formula.

Lord Ian McLaurin, CEO during the growth phase of Tesco, said that the development of the company's revolutionary supermarket concept originated from a detailed X ray of customer needs and the creation of some customer panels regarding the shopping experience. Victor Fung, CEO of Li & Fung, described how "we have learned that most new sources of growth in our business now come from deeper and deeper understanding of the details of our customers. In fact, our whole organization is comprised of teams formed around our major customers."[5] Andy Taylor, CEO of Enterprise Rent-A-Car, also paid strict attention to his customers: "Our core customers are those who rent from us in our neighborhood locations. These customers may rent because their own vehicle is in the repair shop, or they want to take a short business or leisure trip, or need a different car for a special occasion. We have built our services like customer pickup and suburban locations to serve the needs of that specific segment. Even now, our move into airports is geared to the needs of this customer segment that appreciates a higher level of service."[6] Pasquale Pistorio of STMicroelectronics echoed these points: "I insist that we keep total humility about customer knowledge. Almost all of our major new sources of growth have come because of this. When we have diverted to ideas not driven by the customer, like the ST personal computer chip or the PC graphics, we found we did not succeed, because we were not close enough to the customer and could not drive the speed of innovation fast enough without that intimate knowledge."[7]

Throughout the case studies, more than three-quarters of the most successful companies had a repeatable formula, and three-quarters of those that did built the formula around insights related to customer behavior and customer segments. The key insights underpinning all these successful, customer-centric growth formulas originated from a relatively small number of ways to look at customers' needs, each of which is illustrated below with an example. These insights sometimes come from deep market research, which includes such intricate techniques as attaching small cameras to customers or sending out teams to map out customer work flow and problems at the job site.

There are many more techniques, but the purpose of this book is not to catalog these market research methods; those are readily available. It is to demonstrate how new waves of growth beyond the core can sometimes be found by looking deep within the core, what I refer to in this book as the Paradox of Adjacency Expansion.

There are five primary lenses, described in the remainder of this chapter, for looking at a core customer base in search of new forms of profitable growth. These lenses each uniquely focus on the following five dimensions:

- Customer economics and profit drivers

- Customer share of total spending ("share of wallet")

- Customer life cycle of events and purchases

- Customer segmentation

- Customer-based product regimens

Insights from the Customers' Profit Economics

One of the most powerful ways to identify potential adjacency opportunities is through the detailed understanding of the cost and profit economics of key customers. Companies can create expertise in this capability by building organizational skills that allow them to understand the full economics of the customer's business drivers as completely as the customer does. A company may develop a deeper understanding of the customers' most vexing problems than the customers themselves have.

The story of Hilti shows one approach to this angle of attack on growth. As you read on, ask yourself when you have last done something like this with your core customers. Hilti, a Lichtenstein-based company founded in 1941 by Martin Hilti, has focused on sophisticated drilling and fastening techniques for construction since its inception and has now become the world leader in its target market. Since 1995, Hilti has grown revenues at 9 percent to 3.2 billion CHF and earnings at 14 percent to 369 million CHF in a market whose underlying growth rate is about 2 percent. Pius Baschera, CEO of Hilti, has driven a real revival of growth in the company by returning to the original core focus of deep, detailed customer segmentation and deeper and deeper specific applications after a "stall-out period" of low-profit growth. During this stagnant period, the company had tried to move down-market into commodity products, fueling new growth but threatening profitability.

Baschera specifically describes how Hilti goes about finding new product ideas, some of which might be organic within the core, but some of which lead to new adjacencies of a larger scale:

> Our core business is our fastening, drilling, cutting, and positioning technologies. Our expansions have come by adding new, more sophisticated products for our historic core customers and taking the present technologies into new customer segments.
>
> Here is an example of how we do this. In 1996, we went out on job sites with a team of people with expertise in ergonomics and analyzed in detail how our customers do the job. Taking notes and running video cameras constantly, [we were] virtually living with these customers. Our focus was how we could improve productivity on the job site. We analyzed, for example, electricians and how they put on cable trays on the floors and ceilings. We broke down the day of an electrician minute by minute in his activities to set the anchor, identify where to drill, and so on.
>
> We found that the biggest portion of time, 35 percent of the day, is determining where to drill to fix these cable trays, before using our products to do the drilling and fastening itself. The workers were doing the measurement by hand on ladders with measuring bands in a cumbersome process. We determined that laser technology was the answer and searched for an outside supplier, a partner, to develop such a positioning product for our customers. From nothing,

this has grown to a 100 million CHF product line in four years; we have a strong position in this market and are now forming a joint venture for development and manufacturing to grow this segment further. We find that deeper understandings like this lead to insights about the biggest growth opportunities.[8]

If it's relevant to do so in your business, ask yourself how often you have invested resources to visit customer sites, developing a full picture of the customer's needs and economics related to the use of your product. Most companies don't, for it takes energy and resources and is a bit threatening. In failing to make this customer connection, however, most companies leave money on the table.

Insights from Customer Share of Wallet

On average, *share-of-wallet* adjacencies—that is, the selling of highly related products to customers you know intimately—have the highest success rates among adjacency types. On the other hand, ironically, false share-of-wallet theories have seduced many management teams into disaster. Certainly, the annals of adjacency expansions are littered with case studies of companies that built grand strategies on broad, untested, and incorrect theories of customer bundling—Saatchi & Saatchi in consulting, Sears in financial services, and Allegis in travel, to name a few. However, building growth on proven and tested customer behaviors regarding multiple purchases is still one of the best strategies. The issue is how to test, and how to decide, before pushing the investment launch button.

Enterprise Rent-A-Car is one of the most successful family-run businesses in the world. Started by former fighter pilot Jack Taylor in 1957, the company was later named for the USS *Enterprise,* an aircraft carrier he landed on in World War II. Enterprise Rent-A-Car is today a nearly $7 billion business that has grown its rental volume in the past ten years at more than double the rate of the rest of the rental car market. Today Enterprise has the largest private fleet of vehicles in the world, with 625,000 cars, quite a contrast from the fleet of seventeen rental cars assembled in Clayton, Missouri, as an adjacency expansion to car leasing. Enterprise first began renting vehicles in 1962 to its lease customers who needed a replacement vehicle while their automobiles were in the shop being repaired. At the time that it was inventing a new form of neighborhood car rental, there was already a thriving airport rental market for businesspeople. Enterprise avoided this existing segment for decades, focusing almost entirely on building its core business around a new and different segment of customers. And it has done that well, growing its market share in this segment to an overwhelming leadership position within the body shop, insurance, and dealership industries.

So how do you keep growing from this position? The major avenue for Enterprise is by following its core customers into other segments of vehicle use. Enterprise now serves all major airports and is in the terminals of nearly all of the top one hundred airports, where it has gained 5 percent overall market share, focusing as it does on the infrequent renters or cost-conscious business traveler as opposed to the frequent business renters who are the core of Avis and Hertz. As CEO Andy Taylor describes:

> We decided to see whether our core customers would appreciate our higher level of customer service. So we tested it in Denver for a year and followed our customer service scores closely. We found that our core customers did appreciate finding our service at the airport, and so we tailored our airport operations to include things like soft drinks in the vans, greeters with travel recommendations—a very friendly service. This is just one example of how we have listened to our customers and have been led to new opportunities. Another would be our newest division, Enterprise Rent-A-Truck. We have started a commercial truck rental business in thirty-seven locations focused on businesses that have a need for supplemental or replacement trucks, similar to how our

neighborhood rental car business started. Another new adjacency is what we call the "virtual car" concept. We found that people often need a different vehicle other than their own to meet numerous lifestyle and transportation needs. Customers are buying vehicles that meet a majority of their requirements and renting a vehicle to satisfy their remaining needs. This also holds true in cities where owning and housing a car is expensive and a nuisance.[9]

Sometimes, share-of-wallet adjacencies can take a different form: adjacencies that allow more detailed segmentation and penetration of the customer base by cutting it finer and finer, as opposed to (or in addition to) new services and products added on to current customers. A powerful example of this use of adjacency expansion is the last fifteen years of growth experienced by American Express.

Like so many of the companies examined in this book, American Express has a long history and has evolved dramatically over time through the use of adjacencies. American Express began in 1850 as an express package delivery company in New York State. Its well-known product, Travelers Cheques, was first introduced in 1891, one of a series of vehicles that competed with government postal money orders and had valuable application in cashing letters of credit in Europe. During World War I, the government nationalized express delivery services, and American Express remained primarily in its financial products to facilitate commerce and aid travelers. The first American Express charge card was introduced in 1958, changing relatively little until the share-of-wallet adjacency strategy that Ken Chenault developed thirty years later and that played out in the 1990s. The prior decade holds a further lesson for executives thinking about growth. During this time, the company pursued two different share-of-wallet strategies: one "in the large," the other one built up from a detailed understanding of the behavior of legitimate customer segments. The contrast of two share-of-wallet adjacency expansion strategies, one mythical and disastrous, one powerful and successful, defines an almost perfect mirror image.

In the mid-1970s, the American Express card business was extremely profitable. A Harvard Business School case study described what happened next: "But James Robinson III, who became CEO in 1977, had a larger company in mind. His first significant acquisition was Shearson Loeb Rhoades, an innovative and highly successful brokerage house, purchased in 1981 for $1 billion. Over the next six years, Robinson strove to make American Express the largest 'financial supermarket' in the world."[10] In short order, he acquired The Boston Company (for asset management), Trade Development Bank Holdings S.A. (European banking), Investors Diversified Services, First Data Resources (a merchant processor), Lehman Brothers Kuhn Loeb (investment banking), and E. F. Hutton (brokerage). Unfortunately the businesses had no real linkage at all at the customer level in terms of buying in a bundled way, and created little, if any, cost synergies. Instead they created confusion and destroyed value: From 1987 through 1991, the market value of American Express declined by more than 50 percent. In 1992, a new management team led by Harvey Golub and Ken Chenault was put in place.

This time, the company's approach evolved to a share-of-wallet strategy for the card base, a model that Chenault had developed and argued for in prior years without support. But by 1995, after a ten-year period of zero growth in the stock price, the market value had increased by 290 percent. The strategy, built on customer knowledge, had essentially three adjacency elements, each designed to target finer and finer segments of American Express's cardmember base, targeting a higher percentage of the customers' spending through these new instruments more precisely tailored to their needs. One element was the increase in the number of card products beyond the basic American Express green, gold, and platinum charge cards. In a series of moves, the company introduced in 1994 the Optima card as a stand-alone, revolving credit card; in 1996 the Delta Skymiles card, a family of affinity group cards, and a family of special-purpose business cards such as purchasing; and recently the Blue credit card, with special Internet payment features, and the

Centurion (Black) card. The second element of this strategy was the launching of a Membership Rewards program whereby cardholders could earn points for spending, redeemable for products and services. The third component was an aggressive wave of new add-on service initiatives, including credit insurance, travel insurance, life insurance, and baggage insurance, offered to cardholders.

Like many of the best adjacencies, these initiatives have substantial self-reinforcing linkages and spawn other services as a consequence. In other words, these initiatives enjoy repeatability. For example, if a cardholder loses his or her wallet and telephones American Express for a replacement card, the phone operators and the background messages all make the customer aware that for a small fee it is possible to purchase various insurance products and be a member of a comprehensive card registry (a service that will also improve the customer's experience if he loses his wallet again).

American Express has built an effective and repeatable process to seek out, test, and execute on these new adjacencies. It has turned what was not too long ago a single card product for consumers with no add-on services into a sophisticated family of targeted financial instruments, for consumers, small businesses, and large corporations, varying by interest rate, terms, credit limit, associated services, and rewards program features. This approach has driven 12 percent growth, from $14.2 billion in 1993 to $22.6 billion in 2001, with most of this growth coming from increased purchases per customer, or share of wallet.

Insights from Understanding the Customer Life Cycle

One way to identify the potential for share-of-wallet adjacencies is to look across the life cycle of the purchases of an individual customer, searching for linkages among purchases that create a chain of adjacency expansion opportunities. PETsMART, the leading retailer of pet supplies and services in the United States, provides an excellent example of how a strategy built around the concept of life-cycle purchases can lead to a new surge of profitable growth as well as a clearer definition of the business and its growth potential for employees and investors. From 1990 to 2002, the company grew from $188 million in sixteen stores to $2.5 billion in 353 stores, for a 33 percent rate of annual growth. PETsMART is one of the most profitable specialty retail chains, with 2002 EBITDA return on assets of 22 percent and return on equity of 37 percent.

PETsMART was founded in 1987 in Phoenix, Arizona, and expanded dramatically through the 1990s by acquisition of regional chains and by organic expansions of its own stores primarily focused on selling pet food and hard goods for house pets. But in 1998 and 1999, the company began struggling and lost money. The distribution system was outdated, resulting in constant stock-outs at the stores. Because the business had lost touch with its customers and had not studied their needs in depth, customer loyalty started to wane. Information systems were patched together, making forecasting and merchandising impossible. Here is how the current CEO, Phil Francis, describes the situation that caused overstocks in low-turn items and out-of-stocks in the most popular items: "We were flying at night in an airplane with no radar, and no place to land. One phrase popped into my head—impending doom. . . . We had trailers of cat furniture in the back of the store, and no Hill's on the shelf."[11]

The PETsMART management drove a rapid operational turnaround in systems and logistics, but that alone was not enough to reverse the stock price that had plummeted by 70 percent from June 1999 to May 2000. They realized they needed to create an engine of growth. They called the vision they came up with to guide their growth program Total Lifetime Care. The bold new blueprint consisted of three separate operating initiatives to completely change the store format, to upgrade customer service levels in the stores, and to expand the pet services business. The store format project, which became a symbol of the growth strategy, was called Project Eagle, after a $2.50 wooden eagle that Bob Moran, company president and chief operating officer, brought to the meetings of the cross-functional team challenged to redesign the store. The strategy was executed well. Today the stock price has increased into the high teens, from its low of $2.50 just three years ago.

A key element was a unifying vision of the customer, how the store was going to uniquely serve the customer, and where new growth areas would be found. The answer was to focus on those pet owners, "pet parents," who quite literally treat their pets like children and are willing to do almost anything for their well-being. PETsMART would become the place where these people would turn not just for food, but for a full range of services. The target market for this approach is amazingly large. In surveys, 62 percent of pet owners indicate that they relate to pets as they would children. The combined market for services and products serving the 141 million dogs and cats in the United States is $29 billion. PETsMART did extensive analysis of customer needs, perceptions, and buying patterns for everything from food to training to grooming to veterinary services. The more that PETsMART was able to create this bond by consolidating in its stores some of the highly fragmented and inefficient pet services market, the more it would become competitively differentiated from Wal-Mart and grocery stores that could never follow this strategy. Furthermore, this vision would create a string of new product and service adjacencies to explore, repetitively, for a long time. The total universe of possible pet services is extensive, including dietary services, dental services, chiropractic services, aquarium setup, out-of-store pet sitting, diagnostic services, training, grooming, animal health, and even overnight boarding. So far, PETsMART has focused its resources on grooming, training, veterinary services, and a pet hospital alliance with Banfield, and is even testing PETsHOTELs in some of its stores.

David Lenhardt, director of services, says that the services aspect of the business was initially treated as an incidental: "In doing customer segmentation, [we realized that] there was a sizable set of customers who valued a set of services from one place very highly. It was a clearly differentiating approach and had the added benefits of moving towards higher-margin services. Furthermore, we found that we had been offering some services like training and grooming in some stores as a sideline business, a stepchild business, but we had not focused on it as a profit generator, and as an important part of the core business."[12] In 2002, this new service adjacency strategy generated $154 million and is growing at an annual rate of over 20 percent. In a sense, the unifying strategy of PETsMART creates a potential adjacency machine driving into new services for new categories of pets and then driving the most successful ones deeper into the store network. The concept of total lifetime care is something employees and investors can understand and relate to.

The idea of looking at the customer "corridor" of purchases for adjacencies is one that I have seen work in many businesses. The growth of Lloyds Bank is built around an understanding of life-cycle needs of customers buying, for example, their first mortgage and needing soon thereafter a predictable set of new insurance products. However, it is easy to fall into a trap of false enthusiasm with regard to the concept of share of wallet, or customer bundling. Rapid prototyping, testing the key behavioral assumptions rigorously, and then responding rapidly to proven success are key.

Insights from Customer Segmentation

Ask Michael Dell about the key driver of growth, and he'll put customer segmentation right at the top of the list. Segmentation can create new opportunities either by identifying new geographic or customer segments to attack using the direct model, or by taking an existing segment and subdividing it to achieve greater customer focus. "We have virtually organized our whole company around customer segments, and most of our sources of new growth have involved customer segmentation in one way or another."[13]

When Dell first split its public sector activities into education and government, then split education into primary and secondary education, and then split into colleges and universities, the company uncovered major new growth opportunities all along the way. The way it works is that Dell establishes a slightly different version of its direct model with somewhat different sales-force training, a different product focus, and, most importantly, a different sales-force cost structure (such as by varying the mix of direct and indirect salespeople). As long as the company grows, it can continuously subsegment large groups of customers to tailor the model more precisely to their needs in terms of both its economics and service levels.

P&G: From Customer Insights into Repeatable Adjacencies

Procter & Gamble is one of the great companies of the world, beginning with its origins from the merger of a soap maker and a candle maker in Cincinnati in 1837. Its first big product, Ivory, a bar of soap that floated so that you could find it in a tub or lake, was borne of knowledge combined from soap making and candle making. Today, P&G has grown to a $39 billion company with three hundred brands and has a growth challenge: how to continue growing at a rate above the market. P&G makes its living from a set of highly competitive, low-growth markets in which every 1 percent increase in growth requires the company to come up with another $400 million business each year! One answer is through adjacencies. Indeed, one P&G executive referred to the company as "a company of adjacencies" and speculated that turbocharging the P&G model for adjacency expansion was the primary way that sustained, profitable growth would continue.

Certainly, some of the most revolutionary farming techniques have been developed in arid lands where growth is the hardest to achieve. Some of the most powerful technologies in the oil industry relate to the reclamation of oil from long-standing, well-understood wells as opposed to abundant, new gushers. Similarly, some of the most difficult growth environments for business, like the world of consumer products inhabited by P&G, may force companies to rise above their conditions and to push the boundaries of techniques to mine new adjacencies. P&G's ability to consistently find major new growth opportunities from deeper and deeper detailed customer knowledge holds lessons for all.

Though the weighted average growth rate of P&G's markets is only about 2 percent, the company has grown at more than twice the average since 1980, with spurts significantly above that. Some growth has been through acquisition, but more is through driving market share and finding close-in adjacencies around its core products. Just consider the comments A. G. Lafley made in our discussion about the growth potential of the core brands:

> A telling example for me personally is the case of Tide. In 1983, I had been with the company for six years and was given the Tide brand to manage, the company's largest U.S. brand and second largest worldwide. At the time, the market share was twenty-one, and we had discussions up to the chairman of the company about what the right laundry strategy should be. The pressure from above was to diversify into totally new brands and categories. Probably once per decade P&G goes off into a foray of "let's create totally new categories and brands from scratch." Then we return to find growth closer to the core. But, for a while, we milked Tide to pay for these forays into new areas, all of which, of course, failed.
>
> I was a voice crying in the wilderness: Just give me one dollar for every ten spent elsewhere, and I will find growth out of Tide. And we did. Between 1983 and 1993, we had grown Tide from a 21 share to a 30 share and expanded the market. I believe the responsibility of a leading brand is to care for the market and to make sure it does not commoditize. Today the Tide share is 38 in the U.S. and 47 in Canada. A target of 50 is not unreasonable. The basic product has led

to a continuous stream of new adjacent opportunities ranging from Liquid Tide to Tide with Bleach to product upgrades with enzymatic stain remover. Sixty years of Tide and
sixty years of upgrades and expansions from the core. It is
the relentless drumbeat of meaningful news for the person
who launders at home. If the market growth rate is 1 percent, we have coaxed 2 to 4 percent out year after year in
close-in adjacencies in all directions out from the core.

One of the things I love about the laundry business is
how we broke down the steps to create a regimen business.
How do you sort the garments? How do you pretreat the garments, and what can we do there? How do you wash the
garments in the machine? How do you dry the garments?
How do you posttreat the garments? We have products now
all along this chain of use, this regimen. The baby care business is also a regimen business where you can apply this repeatable formula that we learned from Tide. We are just
starting in the skin care business, and I am seeing the same
thing there. Growth of even low-growth categories can be
found in many places when you have this sort of method
that you can apply over and over as well as experiences from
using it to find growth in other applications to draw upon.[14]

Though not true adjacency expansion (as it is within the core
itself), the Tide example does illustrate the power of deep customer
insight in finding pockets of growth. P&G is finding that the same
tools sometimes can lead to much larger, and truly adjacent, opportunities for growth. As a result, the company is using new and
creative ways to capture the benefits from these customer insights.
Many of its approaches to turn its repeatable stream of customer insights into true moneymakers today involve *open-market innovation,*
whereby a business unit fills in missing capabilities by looking outside its four walls into other units in the company or by looking outside the company. In some situations, the more powerful a company's
adjacency machine is at finding new customer-centric opportunities,

the more important it is to recognize that those opportunities may require a well-honed approach that looks outside to fill them.

I have done work with my colleague Darrell Rigby on the topic of open-market innovation in companies. As part of that work, we surveyed two hundred senior executives around the world about their views on innovation. Of these executives, 134 (67 percent) felt that their companies would have a lot to gain from ideas and knowledge available outside their companies, and 114 (57 percent) felt that they were too internally focused in their growth strategies.[15]

Lafley hopes that 50 percent of the new growth at P&G over the next several years will come from tapping sources outside the company in the form of partnerships and acquisitions, and that 30 percent of new product ideas will derive from the outside. One example is Iams, a pet nutrition business purchased in 2001 for $800 million. P&G believed it could create value by building a regimen of product adjacencies bolted onto Iams in areas like pet dental care, pet hair treatment, and pet weight control in much the same way that P&G created value with Tide. The ability to create value through product adjacencies gives P&G a leg up in growing through acquisition with a repeatable pattern of value creation tools. The company applied the same regimen-based strategy to Pantene, a product line acquired in its Richardson-Vicks acquisition, and has similarly built up this adjacency to a profitable $1.8 billion business.

The methods of open-market innovation that P&G now uses to take advantage of its customer-based insights are especially evident in how it grew its Crest dental care business into two large adjacencies, teeth whitening and brushing. The product managers of Crest have followed the P&G approach of creating product variations of toothpaste directly in the core, like Crest with fluoride, or Crest with tartar-fighting properties. Only recently has P&G used the Crest brand as a launch pad to push into true adjacencies in the areas of tooth whitening systems and even disposable electric toothbrushes.

Crest Whitestrips, a tooth whitening system that works by applying thin plastic strips to the teeth for half-hour intervals, was launched in June 2000 at retail. The product idea came from extensive analysis of customer dental desires, and frustration with available methods of whitening, such as expensive in-office treatments or slow-acting whitening toothpaste. Currently, more than half of adults say that they would like to whiten their teeth if they could, but only about 1 percent actually do it. P&G developed its attack on this problem with an exercise to build the specifications of the perfect product based on detailed consumer observation and tests that included digitized whitening of customer teeth and analysis on the exact whiteness levels that consumers in these tests most coveted. The process revealed that the ideal product would involve short applications (say, twenty minutes), something people could do at home; comfort so they could perform normal functions with the product in their mouth; and the need only to whiten the front teeth. In fact, whitening the back teeth is almost dysfunctional. Furthermore, analysis of the physics of whitening revealed that only very small amounts of the hydrogen-peroxide-based gel were really needed.

Given the parameters, the company assembled a cross-functional team, including scientists who were expert at film technology, materials and packaging, and oral care products. Gil Cloyd, chief technology officer for P&G, explained, "We decided to look for a thin, flexible membrane. The corporate lab suggested a material used in food packaging called Impress, which contains small dimples that could be used to hold the peroxide gel, is thin enough and of a substance that could be kept in the mouth comfortably and safely. The team was able to create a prototype in a month and be in small-scale production in three months."[16] This type of collaboration across business units in technical matters now characterizes 70 percent of major new product launches at P&G, much higher than ever before. This form of open-market innovation, creating a free exchange of ideas, will be critical to P&G as it tries to maintain its growth momentum by realizing the stream of customer-centered opportunities that the company generates.

In its first year, the Whitestrips business hit $200 million in sales and is on track to hit $500 million in its second year in North America alone. Product awareness is now up to 80 percent, and personal referrals are starting to kick in, pushing the product into the range of the S-curve that P&G calls the "early majority." This is the fastest product ramp-up at P&G since the early 1980s and the first product ever to make profits even in its test market.

On top of this success in Crest Whitestrips, P&G went further in its pursuit of new growth opportunities built on the strong Crest core and identified through its customer research. The company entered the electric toothbrush business, with a battery driven Crest-branded disposable product. The product is called SpinBrush, the brainchild of some independent inventors in Cleveland. P&G tested the idea thoroughly and became convinced when one focus group of twenty-four people revealed that twenty-three wanted to take the product home and begin using it. The most revolutionary feature was its price—just $5 compared with more than $50 for most other electric toothbrushes. However, also revolutionary for P&G was the way the company allowed the inventors to have unusual latitude in product development, pricing, and even advertising. Two years later, the product is being sold in twenty countries, with revenues of more than $200 million.

P&G is another example of a company that is truly an adjacency machine in terms of its sustained ability to mine its customer base for growth ideas ranging from extensions in the core to totally new adjacencies. As P&G searches farther for larger chunks of new growth, the company is discovering that how it takes advantage of these opportunities requires some new tricks—from cross-business sharing inside P&G to open-market innovation outside its four walls to acquisitions based on the value-creation potential of P&G's adjacency machine applied to the new business.

Repeatability: A Practical Side of Core Competences

In 1990, Gary Hamel and C. K. Prahalad coined the phrase *core competence* and began to shift the dialogue within corporations about the nature of competitive advantage from one primarily focused on market positions of business units to one that also encompasses deep skills that cut across business units. As examples, they cited companies like Honda and Sony. Honda's deep capabilities in power trains and engines are the explanation for that company's ability to compete successfully in cars, motorcycles, and small, off-road vehicles. Sony clearly has a core competence in the ability to design and miniaturize electronic products. This ability runs as a theme through diverse businesses, from camcorders to computers to the Walkman. Hamel and Prahalad posed the question about the right strategic architecture to foster and build these competences that cut across different organizational units within a company, but are often not managed in a focused way. The ideas they offered and the questions they posed triggered a flood of academic writing on the topic.

Hamel and Prahalad provided wide latitude in the definition of a core competence: "Core competencies are the collective learning in the organization. . . . Core competence is about harmonizing streams of technology. It is also about the organization of work and the delivery of value."[17] These are extremely broad guidelines. Some of the CEOs interviewed indicated that the idea of core competence had clearly shaped how they look at the root causes of their competitive advantages, and some even said that it provided a way of thinking about the most important assets of their company. Despite the importance of the core competence idea, however, the CEOs were not sure about how to translate the concept into new growth opportunities, into adjacencies.

Perhaps one of the most practical manifestations of this idea of core competence is the power of repeatable formulas for successful adjacencies. Nike's ability to execute on its repeatable formula for entering new sports without being copied by competitors is based, in part, on the core capabilities that it exercises, adapts, and strengthens every time it applies its approach again. One of those competences is outsourcing, which Nike does with 100 percent of its shoe production. Another competence is in signing and dealing with big-name athletes and then leveraging those associations in its products and marketing. A third competence resides in the details of its brand and image building.

FIGURE 2 - 3

Definition of the Core for Enterprise Rent-A-Car

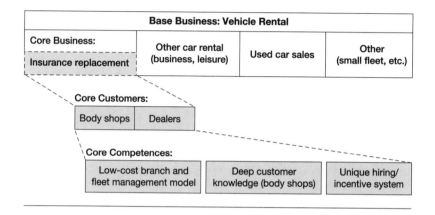

Enterprise Rent-A-Car's success illustrates well how these ideas fit together (figure 2-3). The company's base business is vehicle rental. All the adjacencies the company has pursued build on its success in its core business, which is vehicle rental for replacement purposes, as distinct from business or leisure use, fleet leasing, or any other segments of that market. Body shops are the strongest customer segment within the replacement business. The ability to capture and defend this market segment against attacks from Hertz, Alamo, and others resides in the core competences developed along the way. The first core competence lies in the areas of hiring and personnel management. (Enterprise is the largest hirer of new college graduates in the United States and has strict and creative methods to select the students who are most likely to succeed.) Another significant competence is the company's low-cost suburban branch network. The last core competence is the methods Enterprise employs to manage its vast fleet, now the largest private fleet of vehicles in the world. This lineup of core competences, a loyal core customer, and a dominant core business position is what provides the platform to attack new adjacencies.

Keeping the preceding case examples in mind, management teams concerned with growth might reflect on the following questions:

- Do I have a repeatable formula to find new areas of growth? What is it? Have I really pushed it to its limit?

- How do I describe my growth strategy to the outside world? Do I describe a convincing and repeatable method?

- Do competitors seem to have a repeatable method, or a more convincing case for where their next wave of growth is coming from? Why?

- Am I going in too many growth directions at once, to the point that I would create more value from focusing on a narrower set of methods, perfecting them?

- When is the last time I really invested in examining the true customer segments and their boundaries? The system economics of my best customers by going on-site and doing the analysis? The full share of wallet in all my major customers and what explains it? The potential to develop product regimens that are much more broad and that build on my strongest product franchises?

- How many different adjacency directions am I pursuing, and if they are successful, what will that imply for the complexity of my organization in the future?

Underlying all these questions is the issue of choosing direction and evaluating the true economics of any adjacency strategy or even a single move. Businesses making these judgments have both created tremendous value from a new wave of growth and destroyed value by focusing in the wrong place. It is to these critical judgments that we now turn.

3

Evaluating Adjacency Moves

Balancing Desire with Data

Vodafone, the global leader in the cellular phone business, made its first call from Parliament Square in London on January 1, 1985, to its headquarters fifty miles away. Since then the company has made a lot of good calls, both over the airwaves and in the boardroom. In 1988, Vodafone and British Telecom were the leading regional cellular carriers in the United Kingdom. At this time, the U.K. market had 480,000 subscribers, of which Vodafone had 264,000. By 2003, Vodafone had grown to become the worldwide leader in cellular services, achieving revenues of $50.4 billion, three times the size of its nearest competitor, while British Telecom has exited the business. In spite of the collapse in the telecom sector's market values, Vodafone's stock price has held a strong increase, from $3.88 per share in 1992 to $18.43 ten years later.

Sir Christopher Gent, the current CEO of Vodafone, started with the company, coincidentally, on the same day as its first cellular phone transmission, and he rose internally to his current appointment in 1996. His description of the key forks in the road in the history of Vodafone involved five major adjacency choices that faced the company. Had these decisions been made differently, the management team believes it would not have achieved the level of success it has. The role of major adjacency decisions in the history of Vodafone, and the criteria and process that the company has developed to address them, illustrates many of the key points that emerged from more extensive research presented later in this chapter on the importance of adjacencies and the key success factors.

The first key decision point that Gent describes is a binary choice: "I took over when there was the idea of not only providing the service, but manufacturing the equipment. That would have been a hopeless mistake. We did not have scale or position, and we would be invading the territory of people who supplied us, which is a further problem. This is a good example of a bad adjacency. I made the decision to limit the damage as we exited and sold the [equipment] business to Ericsson. It was the sort of thing that could foul up our strategy in terms of capital, distraction, and management resource."[1]

From 1990 through 2002, Vodafone faced at least four other, similar strategic forks in the road. One was the decision to remain a wireless provider only, to avoid any positions in land-based wireline systems. Many other companies did not follow this path and later regretted it, says Gent. "There was something about global reach for mobile users that was different than for fixed users. We believed there was advantage from single-minded focus on being the best mobile player instead of having the distraction of other things, especially against the advantages of fixed incumbents. It was especially difficult to compete in wire-line systems because of the regulatory constraints under which they operated. So we stayed focused. Paradoxically, we believed it was less safe to be more diverse."

Another fork related to geographic expansion strategy. Should the company expand globally or regionally? How important was local or national leadership? What drove long-term scale economics? Vodafone's analysis indicated that local leadership positions were critical building blocks of the strategy, that regional scale was going to be important, and that the long-term value of global leadership would pay off. As a result, Vodafone targeted leading, or near-leading, positions in various European countries and in the United States through the acquisition of AirTouch, followed by the merger with Mannesmann and with the U.S. business of Verizon, which provided them with leadership in over fifteen other markets. "We come from a legacy of national competitors participating in national markets," says Gent. "They had a high level of resistance to letting their customers go. What we have done is elevate the importance of seamless service and demonstrate the savings that could be made from doing it once and replicating it across the network, making a religion of the best practices. We are now starting to see the real benefits of thinking internationally about scale. This was a critical choice for us."

Whether to sell through distributors or take the risk of setting up Vodafone retail stores to sell directly to the customer was another decision point, says Gent: "As the cellular business evolves into sophisticated data services, it becomes much more important to have direct customer control and understanding of customer spending, usage, requirements, and desires. We need this to make these highly personal devices come alive through the extensions we are making to our base business. The decision to own retail outlets is another adjacency in pursuit of providing a more comprehensive service and bringing our brand into the high street."

Vodafone's history shows consistent success in making the right adjacency choices. As a result of the number of these decisions that constantly seem to emerge in the cellular business, Vodafone's management holds an annual event called the Brocket Hall meetings, at the former home of prime ministers, located outside of London. The sessions focus on these key choices regarding business adjacencies. Sometimes, the most important decisions are to refrain from pursuing an adjacency. During the Internet bubble period, Vodafone was bombarded with opportunities to invest in portals, including the chance to purchase Yahoo! Not being able to make the math work, the company declined them all. Julian Horn-Smith, chief operating officer of Vodafone, explains some of these decisions:

"In the heyday, we avoided a lot of decisions that could have been destructive. A lot of people seemed to be losing their heads. We had bankers asking why we would not buy Yahoo! But if you go through this, you find no barriers to entry, an unproven commercial proposition. It is not being ultraconservative, but insisting on getting the basics right. The main lesson learned is to maintain discipline and keep your head, while everyone around you is losing theirs. People get the impression since we are a new industry that we do not have to be as rigorous. Quite the opposite is true."[2]

To deal with the constant series of major forks in the road, Vodafone has honed, in its Brocket Hall meetings, a decision process that pays particular attention to three dimensions, all of which will emerge as the dominant themes of this chapter:

- Leadership economics and market control in the new adjacencies (e.g., the geographic strategy and the entry into retail)

- A robust profit pool (e.g., the suspicion regarding wire-line investments)

- A clear sense of relatedness to a strong core (e.g., the avoidance of a portal investment)

Adjacency moves are business journeys into the unknown. Each has its strong advocates who, as one executive said to me, can "read poetry to each other all day" in off-site strategy meetings on growth. The list of possible criteria is long. Just from our interviews, we found no fewer than twenty economic criteria listed across a sample of the best CEOs who were asked for their top three.

So, maybe this means that criteria are not that important, that the subconscious brain of the executive will take all this in and let pure instinct take over. I found the opposite. The most successful growth companies, like Dell, Vodafone, Lloyds TSB, Centex Homes, P&G, Hilti, UPS, Tesco, and Staples, insisted on the most rigorous criteria for deciding what to pursue, and especially what not to pursue. While all the companies looked at a lot of data, each had a relatively short list of clear, agreed-upon criteria that the company determined were right for it.

The average strong core business has typically eighty to 110 possible adjacent moves surrounding it at any one time. Perhaps the firm actually evaluates fifteen to twenty of these per year, not including the dozens of investment bank proposals and smaller company approaches that randomly wash up on the beach and are dismissed quickly. Deciding how to decide is crucial in order to avoid mere expediency or excessive complexity or even pure guesswork hidden in the cloak of executive decisiveness. The best companies have honed their criteria and processes for adjacency decisions to military precision.

The most successful companies at adjacency expansion have some of the most restrictive criteria. Is it just conservatism, or is there more at work here? I think it has nothing to do with conservatism per se. Some companies with the most rigorous and clear requirements, like Dell, STMicroelectronics, UPS, and Lloyds TSB, cannot be accused of sidestepping risks or being uncreative in how they have grown their business. So, what is their secret?

One common attribute across most companies with the most evolved decision processes for growth is experience with periods of both strong success and disappointment. It is as if their experiences with revenue stall-out or earnings crises have been definitive and shaping, resulting in more cold-eyed criteria for pursuing growth initiatives. For example, ten years after its disastrous entry into the traditional retail channel, Dell again entered retail. Yet, this time, it did so with kiosks to display product and a mechanism to order through its direct model, not using stocks of inventory and costly layers of distribution. But what is interesting is that Dell's description of its new initiative hearkened back explicitly to the lessons learned from the earlier experience: "The company says it learned its lesson about stocking stores with PC's in the early 90's when it tried to sell through Wal-Mart Stores Inc.'s Sam's Club, Staples Inc., and CompUSA."[3]

Another factor at play is the explicit recognition that rationality in human decision making is inherently imperfect. This is especially true for emotion- and ego-laden decisions such as whether to pursue an exciting, new growth opportunity. One of the definitive studies of rationality, the book *Ulysses and the Sirens,* uses as its dominant metaphor the request made by Ulysses to his crew in the *Odyssey:* "But you must bind me hard and fast, so that I cannot stir from the spot where you will stand me . . . and if I beg you to release me, you must tighten and add to my bonds." Ulysses shows an understanding of his own potential to act irrationally when confronted with the Sirens' songs. The companies best able to pursue growth opportunities are equally aware of the need to impose rules and structure on their own decision-making process.

The Three Pillars of a Successful Adjacency Expansion

How important, really, are strategic choices regarding adjacency expansion, given all the different factors that shape the life of a company? Do they really shape the fortunes of a business, like the case of Vodafone, as much as the CEO interviews suggest? And, if so, what are the most consistent dimensions on which successful and unsuccessful paths differ? Or, alternatively, does success stem primarily from other factors like talent, luck, competitor failures, or external events?

A survey years ago by Bain & Company indicated that about 70 percent of managers who experienced a significant improvement or decay in their business felt that the primary drivers of their fortunes were controllable management decisions. Unlike with the natural sciences, it is impossible in business to run pure prospective experiments to isolate cause and effect. We are left with the ambiguity inherent in sifting through the lessons of the past. This section presents the results from a study of twelve pairs of companies that had similar starting points but different financial trajectories over the ensuing ten years. The intention was to use these "natural experiments" to examine the real importance of choice of adjacency and to identify the most telling determinants of success or failure.

We chose the company pairs (listed in the appendix) through an extensive screening of data to find pairings that exhibited different performance from a similar starting point and that could be isolated and studied closely through available public data.[4] This was not a witch-hunt for disasters, but a search for widely different trajectories from 1990 to 2001. The two groups, the fast and slow value creators, started in similar total positions (we summed up the twelve companies' figures to get the totals):

	Fast Group	Slow Group
Revenue	$59 billion	$78 billion
Operating income	$5 billion	$6 billion
Valuation at start	$49 billion	$43 billion
Increase in value	9.7-fold	3.4-fold
Value created	$427 billion	$102 billion

What can explain such different results from similar starts? Each company's adjacency moves were charted from news articles, press releases, public financial statements, and analyst reports. My team supplemented this information with calls to the company and discussions with industry experts. In total, these twenty-four companies identified more than five hundred major adjacency moves over an average of ten years, about two per year per company. We also cataloged these by type of move (e.g., international expansion, acquisition, entry to a new channel) and relatedness to the current core business.

Despite diverging financial trajectories, both the slow and fast value creators were active in making moves. It was not as if we chose one set of companies that did nothing and another set that was constantly taking action. The slow value creators made an average of sixteen observable moves, and the fast value creators made an average of twenty-one moves. There were also no significant differences in the percentage of moves that were by acquisition, or in other gross measures like that. The differences were in the following three factors:

1. The way the companies built on their core strengths

2. The economics of the markets the companies attacked

3. The extent to which they built positions of leadership economics in the new adjacencies

Across these twelve paired comparisons and our interviews, these three factors appeared repeatedly. In itself, the list of these factors contains no dramatic new revelations. Yet, most companies have not achieved mastery, and this is where the leverage is. There is a reason that Ben Hogan's *Five Lessons: The Modern Fundamentals of Golf* sticks to the basics and why most golf pros contend that getting the few basics right is still where most golfers have the greatest potential for improvement. Moreover, such basic judgments are extremely difficult for even the most experienced managers to make correctly. My hope is to provide some facts, case examples, and ideas that management teams can use in these decisions. Some companies have proven strong records at making these judgments over many years and industry investments. Useful insights can be gleaned by understanding what these companies do. Three pillars for evaluating growth opportunities are described in the following sections.

Success Factor One: The Best Adjacencies Build on and Reinforce the Strongest Cores

Relatedness to a strong core is the most powerful and reliable engine of value creation by pushing out the boundaries of your business. In seven of the twelve pairs of companies we studied, the slower value creator clearly moved away from this basic principle to its peril relative to the faster value creator.

The exhortation to build on and reinforce unique strengths sounds obvious. Yet, it is surprising how many massive adjacency investments and strategies founder on false premises. You only have to go back and read the press clippings to feel the adulation for Mattel when it bought The Learning Company for $3 billion as its foray into the digital age. Within two years, the business had collapsed and was sold to a financial buyer for a price of zero, demonstrating that it had virtually no relationship to Mattel's core toy business. The same was true of Baxter Healthcare's acquisition of American Hospital Supply, the leader in distribution, only to spin it off a decade later, having lost competitive position, because the perceived synergy between Baxter's original core supply manufacturing business and distribution was illusory. Merck spun off its distribution investment in Medco in 2002, announcing its newfound belief that the businesses would perform better apart than together, at exactly the time that analysts were becoming more concerned about the scale and reinvestment rate in Merck's pharmaceutical business. My team collected more than one hundred examples of major investments made on unsubstantiated assumptions about the true relationship between the new adjacency and the initial core business. So while it may sound obvious, this first adjacency rule is violated often and at great peril.

Tesco Versus Sainsbury

The comparison of two, once-similar, grocery businesses, Tesco and Sainsbury, shows how companies in our paired comparisons followed distinct paths, relatively quickly, to different outcomes. Tesco and Sainsbury are grocery companies in the United Kingdom in head-to-head competition with virtually the same starting positions. In 1990, Tesco had a market capitalization of $3.1 billion; Sainsbury had $4 billion. Tesco's revenues were $7.4 billion to Sainsbury's $8.6 billion. Profit margins and P/E ratios of the stock prices were nearly identical. Even the history of each is strangely similar. Tesco started in 1932 as a chain of London grocery stores founded by World War I veteran Jack Cohen. Sainsbury began as a small dairy shop in London in the home of the Sainsbury family in 1869, moving into groceries after World War I to meet the growing demand for preserved products.

During the eleven years for which we studied the two companies, each made twenty-four separate adjacency moves to build growth on its original core business. So, both were quite active. Yet, the results differ markedly. Tesco quadrupled in market value, while Sainsbury increased its value by only 35 percent, far less than the average of even the stock market as a whole. Tesco grew its revenues at a 14 percent annual rate, while Sainsbury grew at 9 percent. The profit performance differences were more dramatic still, as Tesco tripled its total earnings whereas Sainsbury's hardly increased at all.

According to our evaluation and to reports by analysts who followed the industry closely, the difference in performance was influenced strongly by two factors. The first was the unique retail model that Tesco had developed and refined based on deep customer research and feedback. The differentiating features ranged from detailed operating policies such as store size and guaranteed checkout time to a strategy of focusing heavily on edge-of-town locations eschewed by other major food retailers, to a heightened emphasis on the freshness of its produce. Beyond the store model, however, the sequence of growth moves was also quite distinct. Sainsbury grew faster and farther from its (apparently weaker) core. For instance, it invested in a hundred-store chain in Egypt, purchased from Ladbrokes a chain of do-it-yourself stores called Texas, and also invested heavily in a new business called Homebase, another chain of do-it-yourself stores. The company is now exiting both businesses. By contrast, Tesco, after some initial disasters in expansion in Ireland and France, decided to invest resources to strengthen and differentiate its core retail model before turning back later to adjacency expansions.

When Tesco did turn to adjacencies, they were tightly bonded onto a newly strengthened core. One set of moves consisted of product expansions into in-store pharmacies, optical product stations, fuel for automobiles, selected kitchen products, and coffee shops in stores. In 1978, Tesco created a method to probe customer needs and track satisfaction through surveys and customer panels that the company continued to refine. Lord Ian McLaurin, CEO of Tesco at the time (now chairman), describes how the method evolved:

> The key to our model was "Keep it simple, stupid." We knew
> we were a supermarket and only invested in things that we

could prove our customers really wanted. We were leaders in doing customer research, asking, "What do you want from the shopping experience?" The same list came up all the time, like petrol, coffee shops, greater freshness, or easy parking. So, we decided to invest all of our money in these areas in improving the model or extending it into new areas. In one case we found that mothers actually did not like the fact that we had sweets at the checkout counter, because of the reaction it caused in their children. Though we were making money on it, we decided to stop selling sweets in that way, because of this customer reaction. That is how we have operated both in the stores and in our decisions on growth moves.[5]

This focused approach has served to increase the throughput and economics of each retail location on average, creating more of a repeatable formula at the same time.

McKesson Versus Cardinal

Consider also the case of McKesson Corporation versus Cardinal Health. In this example, a loosely related adjacency move by McKesson proved especially damaging because it came during a vicious competitive battle for leadership in its tough core market against Cardinal Health. The problem adjacency move diverted resources and attention from the increasingly desperate needs in its wholesale drug-distribution business.

McKesson's origin is traceable to a Manhattan drugstore started by John McKesson in 1833. Through many ups and downs, including a 1941 bankruptcy, the company remained in drug distribution. By 1990, McKesson had grown to become an $8 billion corporation with undisputed leadership in the distribution of drugs to hospitals, pharmacies, and nursing homes in North America. Drug distribution has numerous adjacency opportunities surrounding it in the $110 billion health care supply management market and the $140 billion direct drug distribution market. And until 1998, taking advantage of these opportunities is exactly what McKesson did. Its textbook adjacency expansions included a 1997 investment in the leading Mexican drug distributor; the 1997 acquisition of General Medical, the leading home-care health supply company; and some investments in new capabilities such as pharmacy productivity consulting, automated dispensing systems, and managed prescription drug programs. These actions expanded McKesson's market value by mid-1998 to an all-time high of $18.5 billion, fifteen times its value just eight years earlier. The company was a leader in its core business, was expanding into new surrounding adjacencies, had grown to $30 billion in revenues, and enjoyed an all-time-high operating income of $580 million in a tough, low-margin business.

Maintaining its position competitively was not easy. In 1988, smaller rival Cardinal Health decided to divest its businesses outside of drug distribution to focus its investments in a single business, targeting McKesson's stronghold. Through aggressive acquisitions, Cardinal grew from $700 million in 1988 (less than 10 percent the size of McKesson) to $5.8 billion in 1994, buying strong regional players and assembling their strengths, region by region. In addition, the company began to distinguish itself through an adjacency expansion strategy into services that could help its customers manage pharmaceutical dispensaries and its suppliers' package drugs for distribution more effectively. One example is the 1998 acquisition of Pyxis, a $202 million revenue business that was the leader in point-of-use systems to automate the handling of pharmaceuticals delivered by Cardinal to its customers.

By 1998, in part through acquisitions and in part through market share gain due to service, Cardinal had closed much of the market share gap with its larger rival. As Cardinal gained momentum, McKesson seemed unable to mobilize to stop it. As early as 1991, *Barron's* could see the writing on the wall: "Cardinal's growth record is indeed impressive. For openers, it reflects the original decision to go into the rapidly expanding drug distribution industry. While that industry's sales growth has been averaging about 13 percent per year, Cardinal's internal growth rate has been 50 percent above average, or about 20 percent per year. Acquisitions will push the rate even higher. The company's profit growth, more than 20 percent a year, also has been way above average."[6] McKesson was certainly not inactive, but was somewhat asleep at the switch in this competitive dynamic.

But the key event was a sharp turn in McKesson's adjacency growth strategy when it bought the medical software company HBO & Company for $12 billion in stock. This $1.4 billion company was the leader in systems software to hospitals. At the time of the deal, the companies announced that the new corporation, McKesson HBOC, expected to grow total earnings by 35 percent per year over the next few years. Yet, investors did not buy it. The *Wall Street Journal* cited analysts who "criticized the idea of a link-up, saying the two companies, besides being in health care, had little in common." They proved to be right.

The stock price of McKesson quickly dropped from $83 to $63 per share. When the Securities and Exchange Commission found accounting irregularities that inflated HBO's stated results, investors concluded that McKesson truly did not understand what it had bought. The press coverage at the time reflected this conclusion: "The purge and allegations of highly unethical accounting tactics at the acquired formerly HBO & Company, deflated one of the industry's biggest business-success stories, one that some analysts have long felt was too good to be true. And it leaves McKesson, the nation's top drug distributor, which paid $12 billion for HBO, with a mess that could take years to fix and a new senior management roster that is untested."[7] Immediately the stock slipped another 68 percent to a low of $20 per share in October 1999. Certainly the cost of acquisition was great, the investment characteristics devastating, the subsequent removal of the CEO and CFO disorienting and distracting.

The biggest cost of all for McKesson, however, may have been in the shifting momentum that this adjacency move allowed competitively in drug distribution. Cardinal Health put further fuel to the fire in its expansion program, really pulling away from a distracted McKesson. Cardinal soon bought the number five industry player,

Bindley Western. By 2001, Cardinal had made twenty-nine acquisitions in highly related adjacencies in health-care distribution and in several other key service areas that could serve its primary customers and suppliers. These adjacency and consolidation strategies worked well, but the key element above all may have been its rival's alternative choice of investment paths.

Assessing Distance from the Core

Many of the most successful growth companies were able to maintain strong, highly measurable and mutually reinforcing economics between the current business and the new adjacencies. Similarly, many of the most disappointing case studies, even those that seemed to have all the right initial ingredients for success, foundered because the link to the core was illusory. So how can a management team objectively assess true relatedness between a number of different opportunities and the real core strengths?

One framework that we have found useful in client situations is to think of the *economic distance* between the core business and the potential adjacency. Economic linkages between the existing business and new adjacencies generally increase the odds of success. The linkages create a multiplier effect on performance, with benefits accruing to the existing business from the adjacency and to the adjacency from the existing business.

The distance from an adjacency to the core business can be measured by shared economics. Each business can develop its own tailored measure, but a good starting point is as follows. For each of the following five dimensions, determine whether the growth investment has characteristics identical, or only somewhat similar, to the base business:

- *Customers:* Are they the same as, or different from, those currently served?

- *Competitors:* Are they the same as, or different from, those currently encountered?

- *Cost structure:* Is the cost structure (infrastructure) the same or different?

- *Channels of distribution:* Are these the same or different?

- *Singular capability:* If there is a singular capability (brand, asset, technology) that gives the core business its uniqueness, then is this relevant in the new opportunity?

If the characteristics are identical, then the distance from the core is zero. If the characteristics are only somewhat similar, then estimate the extent of the difference in terms of steps away from the core, say, one-half or three-quarters of a step away. Then add up the total as one measure of distance. For the purpose of this analysis, we will say that the maximum is five and the minimum is zero steps away. If the total is much less than a step away, then the new opportunity is essentially part of the base business, not a real adjacency as we are defining it here.

In several analyses, we found that the odds of success declined precipitously as an adjacency moved two or more steps away from the core business's greatest strengths. Figure 3-1 shows this pattern of declining odds. It is almost as if, two to three steps from the core, there is a zone in which enough is known about the new opportunity to generate enthusiasm, but not enough is known to guarantee that the really tough questions will be asked, let alone answered. Moving farther out, four or five steps away, there is commonly an understanding, that the investment is an unrelated diversification, with all of the usual risks this entails. This zone of uncertainty, from about one and a half to three and a half steps away from the core, is a "trap of false enthusiasm." Many companies enter this trap thinking that the adjacency is more related than it really is. It is as if this is an area in which you can know enough to be excited about an idea, but sometimes not enough to know the tough question, a misperception that can sometimes be most costly.

One senior executive team to whom I recently spoke debated vigorously among themselves about this concept of steps away from the core. They concluded that had they applied this simple screen

FIGURE 3 - 1

Success Declines with Distance from the Core

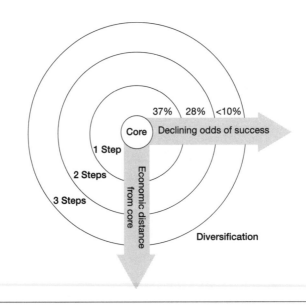

and thought about the statistical record of investments two to three steps away, they probably would have asked much tougher questions about the largest single investment they had ever made. Instead, the investment turned out to be the biggest single economic disaster (more than $1 billion of lost value) in their history of over a century in the same business. Another client asked us to develop a weighted measure of distance for his company's core business and apply it to all current and past growth initiatives. We found almost a perfect inverse correlation between economic success and the distance from the core using this simple method, an exercise that has led to a new way to evaluate and compare growth options.

Assessing the relative distance of different adjacencies is useful in comparing investments to each other as well as in evaluating them on an absolute basis. This certainly does not mean that companies should avoid investments many steps away from their best businesses. On the contrary, all companies should have an organized process to experiment at the boundaries and to plant new seeds. What it does mean, however, is that executive teams should be aware of their investment portfolio and be wary if more than 10 to 15 percent of resources are being invested many steps away from the strongest cores. Companies mentioned earlier, like Mattel, Loral, and McKesson, fell into this trap by making huge investments that turned out to be farther away from their cores than they had realized or allowed themselves to recognize.

Success Factor Two: Drive Adjacencies Toward the Most Robust Profit Pools

Mort Topfer, former vice chairman of Dell and now a member of its board of directors, says this about the company: "We manage according to the principles of profit pools." Remarkably, by 2003, Dell had captured about 100 percent of the profit pool in the personal computer industry, even though it had only 24 percent U.S. market share and 14 percent global market share. Five of our twelve paired comparisons were heavily influenced by differences in how the industry profit pools eventually evolved.

A *profit pool* is different from a market.[8] A profit pool evaluation is designed to embody the size of the industry, its current and potential profit dollars, and the extent to which those earnings could cover the cost of capital for the leading players. Some industries, like the airline industry, have decade-long histories of not earning their cost of capital, with the exception of companies with highly specific ways to segment the market, lower their costs, and create profitability. The prism of profit pools is the way to view the fundamental attractiveness of a market, given its size, growth rate, economic structure (capacity conditions and competitive conditions), and customer alternatives. Sometimes, a new competitive model (e.g., Dell's low-cost model and the premium product and price model of Starbucks) can create new profit pools where none existed before. However, creating a profit pool in a dog-eat-dog industry through a "new model" is the historical exception, not the rule. When it occurs, the reason is usually a dramatic new way to lower costs, thereby producing profits where none previously existed.

British Aerospace Versus Marconi

Marconi and British Aerospace (BAE) are two British companies with similarly long and storied histories, but extremely different fates because of their adjacency moves. In contrast to BAE, Marconi made a dramatic bet on an industry whose profit pool was about to collapse.

In 1990, BAE was nearly twice as large as Marconi (then called GEC) but only half as profitable. But how fast this situation changed! One decade later, Marconi had embarked on a failed adjacency strategy, pursuing a profit pool in telecommunications that proved to be a mirage. BAE had purchased the original core of Marconi in its own adjacency expansion in the defense business, nearly tripling its stock price in five years—from $131 to $334 per share—as Marconi collapsed in value by more than 95 percent. Few adjacency stories have this drama, and few are as closely linked to alternative points of view on future profit pools.

How could this have happened? Marconi grew from a dual lineage—one stemming back to the 1886 start-up of the General Electric Apparatus Company, a distributor of electrical components, and the other emerging from the Wireless Telegraph and Signal Company, which formed in 1897 around the Nobel Prize–winning wireless radio inventions of Guglielmo Marconi. The modern era of Marconi was triggered in 1963, when Lord Arnold Weinstock began his thirty-three-year reign over the combined company, GEC. By the end of his tenure, GEC was a diffuse conglomerate in products ranging across lifts, wire, cables, semiconductors, defense electronics, and many other sectors. The company was underperforming its peers and desperately needed focus, cost reduction, restructuring, and a face-lift. The new management team, led by Lord George Simpson, took its charter seriously, completing twenty-two divestitures and twenty-one acquisitions in three years, starting in 1998. The divestitures even included the core Marconi defense electronic business to BAE for $10.7 billion, providing fuel for the acquisitions in telecommunications equipment—a new business area for Marconi. The *Financial Times* wrote: "Criticisms that the new team wantonly interfered with a successful formula are misplaced. Action was required, and it would undoubtedly entail risks. Moving out of moribund or unfashionable sectors into ones that carry the promise of faster growth is a tricky business. The trick is to get a good price for the company's past, while avoiding overpaying for its future. Lord Simpson and Mr. Mayo did a good job on the first part. They disentangled the old GEC with admirable skill and speed. The problem came in building a new focused business."[9]

Simpson has since been replaced, another example of the high percentage of CEO departures linked to failed adjacency strategies. In this case, there are many apparent causes for failure, but the three that loom largest are the collapse of the profit pool on which Marconi had literally bet everything, a tendency to buy businesses that were not leaders and that were especially vulnerable to the downturn, and a feverish spending spree that reduced the business leaders' ability to think about the fit among adjacencies in telecom as well as the ability to absorb the change.

By contrast, BAE has had a limited revival in spite of tough economic times. From 1995 to 2002, BAE increased its revenues by 123 percent to £12.8 billion, and its operating profit by 271 percent to £1.3 billion. The addition of the Marconi defense electronics business made BAE the most complete defense company in the world, the number one U.K. and European defense company, and one of four global leaders in military aircraft. The acquisition of Marconi's defense business both represents a move into one of the fastest-growing areas of defense and strengthens its overall systems capabilities in defense electronics and avionics. BAE, it appears, has benefited from a solid and growing profit pool with leadership potential. At the same time, Marconi has had the misfortune of placing all its bets on the shrinking and unstable telecommunications profit pool, with a portfolio consisting mostly of businesses that are not the leaders in their sector—a tough place to be.

Mapping the Profit Pool

One of the top developments in the extraction of oil from the earth's surface is four-dimensional geological imaging that allows visualization of pools of oil through the course of drilling and pumping. The ability to follow the petroleum in such a specific sense has led to further developments, such as the ability to drill horizontally from a vertical shaft in pursuit of black gold. Without such imaging, oil companies were left to an almost hunt-and-peck method of sinking wells, studying the basic formations and core samples, and hoping for the best.

Profit pools in business are obviously not as stable and knowable in the future as a deposit of gold or a reservoir of crude oil. However, that does not mean that the attempt to map those pools and anticipate their formation in the future is in vain.

As mentioned, five of our twelve paired comparisons had dramatic differences in profit pool dynamics. Aetna departed from its weak positions in traditional insurance (not a bad move at all) to move aggressively into adjacencies targeting HMOs, an evaporating profit pool. Duke Energy saw the potential for massive, rich profit pools in traditional energy businesses such as natural gas and pipelines, creating an integrated energy company. At the same time, seventy-two deregulated utilities were investing in telecommunications, which were both a distant adjacency from the utilities' core and a profit pool whose collapse stunned even the most sophisticated observers of that industry. Marconi made one of the biggest telecom bets of all, leaving itself extremely vulnerable while also trying to understand and integrate a far-flung array of companies purchased in less than three years, many not in leadership positions. Cardinal Health saw a wide range of adjacent profit pools targeted by its focused strategy on drug distribution, handling, packaging, and management. On the other hand, McKesson became disenchanted with the potential in the same business in which it once was the leader. The company shifted into a temporarily more fashionable, but ultimately less profitable, profit pool of health-care software.

In mapping out a profit pool, it is first necessary to decide on the definitions and boundaries of the relevant markets. These could be defined by geography, stage in the value chain, current owner, product, end user, time phase, channel, or distance from the relevant core business. In addition, it is important to think about what constitutes profit. Is it pure dollars, or is it dollars earning more than the cost of capital? Is it potential profit under a new economic model? Just asking these questions of a growth initiative can be quite clarifying.

Once the definition has been decided on and information has been assembled, it is worth considering the full range of profit pool effects that come into play:

- The direct profit pool entered by the adjacency move

- The impact of the adjacency move back on potential profitability of the core business

- The impact of the core business on the adjacency

- The option value of the move in creating further opportunities

- Profit pools of customers, suppliers, or complementary products

Success Factor Three: Insist on the Potential for Leadership Economics

The decision to make a major investment to push out the boundaries of a core business into an adjacent area requires a clear view of the reinvestment and cash requirements in the future. If you do not have the potential to ever achieve economics equivalent to the leader, then you may be constantly out-invested or put in a position of having to match the leader's investment to achieve lower returns. It is easy to fall prey to this trap of incremental profits, because of the short-term pressures on management teams described earlier.

The long-term cost of short-term decision making in complex environments that push the boundaries of human judgment has been primarily studied in the public sector, where decisions are more openly documented and, so, can be dissected by historians. One of the most scrutinized and revealing cases is the sequence of decisions that led the United States further and further down the path of the Vietnam War. Robert S. McNamara, secretary of defense during the war, wrote a remarkably revealing book on the decisions made. "We were wrong, terribly wrong. We owe it to future generations to explain why. . . . I do so at the risk of oversimplification. One reason the Kennedy and Johnson administrations failed to take an orderly, rational approach to the basic questions underlying Vietnam was the staggering variety and complexity of other issues we faced. Simply put, we faced a blizzard of problems, there were only twenty-four hours in a day, and we often did not have time to think straight."[10]

Certainly, the decisions regarding how to grow a corporation are usually, though not always, at a level of complexity below the issues that McNamara faced regarding Vietnam. However, the pressures on the human mind, and its limitations, are very similar. Study after study has shown how groups under stress retreat to their prior beliefs, shield themselves from conflicting data, focus on just getting through the week or the day, and increasingly surround themselves with people who think like they do. The greater the pressure, the greater the tendency for these reactions to occur. It happens in government, it happens in religious organizations, it happens in spades in corporations.

The importance of a balanced, externally oriented decision process leading to investment in areas that can attain the right long-term economics was reinforced by how the weaker performer allowed itself to be lured into investments in clear follower positions without leadership economics in eight of the twelve paired comparisons. In several cases, like Eckerd Drug and Walgreens discussed in the next section, the weaker performer followed a strategy that did not seem to acknowledge the full set of drivers for leadership economics. In other cases, like Swissair or Marconi, the weaker performer made significant equity investments in companies that were weak followers.

Walgreens Versus Eckerd Drug

The divergent paths of Eckerd Drug and Walgreens show what can happen when one competitor follows the rules of leadership economics better than the other. During the last five years of the period we examined, from 1996 to 2001, both Eckerd Drug and Walgreens grew significantly. Eckerd grew from $3.3 to $9.7 billion in revenues, and Walgreens grew from $7.4 to $19.7 billion in revenues. Yet, for Walgreens, profits surged ahead even more, while Eckerd sagged with declining margins. What happened? Analysis revealed that though Eckerd grew faster on a national basis, the real source of leadership economics is regional relative market share and local density. Despite its penetration strategy during this growth spurt (Eckerd grew faster than Walgreens did), Eckerd spread itself more thinly through small acquisitions. It also drove down its average relative market share compared to its next largest local competitor from 1.0 times (parity) to 0.84 times (behind). At the same time, Walgreens grew organically in denser clusters and increased its average relative market share from 1.1 times to 1.6 times. Typically, the difference in a relative market share of 1.0 (parity) to 1.6 is worth 3 to 6 percent additional return on investment, a huge difference in a competitive battle. This relationship also holds in the case of retail drugstores and almost completely explains the continual widening of the profitability gap between the two companies.

The true power of leadership economics resides most often in the ability to generate higher margins through lower unit costs.

Studies at Bain & Company have found that 80 percent of the difference between a leader's profits and those of a more distant follower is due to unit cost levels. Since most businesses are not leaders, other ways to compete economically and come close to leadership economics (allowing reinvestment) are critical. For example, we found in a group of thirty-three industries and 185 competitors that about 30 percent of the businesses were leaders or had clear leadership economics. Moreover, this 30 percent accounted for 55 percent of revenues (since they were more successful than average), 78 percent of profitability, and 94 percent of the "excess" profits above the cost of capital (read reinvestment capability).

EAS: A Healthy Path to Growth

When all three adjacency success factors hold at once, new, profitable growth usually is worth pursuing, given organizational capacity to execute. The recent growth performance of the active lifestyle nutrition company EAS is an example of how these mutually reinforcing factors signaled the chance to reignite growth after a temporary stall-out.

The original core of EAS began in the mid-1980s at Gold's Gym in Venice Beach, California. It was there that Bill Phillips, a successful competitive bodybuilder, was becoming increasingly concerned with the use of steroids and other performance-enhancing substances by his fellow weight lifters. His disillusionment drove him to begin writing a newsletter called *Natural Nutrition* to promote more natural supplements and alternatives. The newsletter took off, spreading from southern California nationwide, and Phillips began receiving requests for his own formulations. Out of commitment to his cause, he began to distribute the supplements and meal replacements that he himself used, directly from his basement to other bodybuilders.

As revenues mounted, Phillips moved a step further into innovative products for weight management and muscle enhancement, and EAS (Experimental and Applied Science) was born. Phillips was the first to commercialize these products with clear information, testimonials, direct distribution, and a brand. Among the testimonials were the top players from the Denver Broncos football team (including John Elway and Shannon Sharpe) during the two consecutive years, 1998 and 1999, when the Broncos won the Super Bowl. The addition of these endorsements to the mix propelled EAS in 1995 to over $100 million in revenues in 1998, which were heavily reliant on two core products sold mostly to avid bodybuilders and athletes. In the late-1990s, Phillips became increasingly focused on writing his new book, *Body for Life,* and on the contests and teaching surrounding it. This resulted in the company's growth slowing and flattening out at about $155 million in 1999 and 2000. It was then that Northcastle Partners, a private equity company specializing in growing health-related businesses, purchased a majority interest in the company and installed an experienced CEO, Dave Lumley, to revive growth. In his first months, Lumley talked to every manager and salesperson, visited top customers and suppliers, replaced twenty-three of the top forty managers, and learned what drove the business.

At an off-site meeting held near the headquarters in Golden, Colorado, Lumley, the management team, and Northcastle boiled down his findings and supporting market research into an adjacency strategy that they referred to as moving from "the island to the mainland." The island was the strong core of nutritional science and loyal, avid bodybuilder customer franchise (a market potential of about five million people). The mainland was the much larger group of people committed to improving their bodies or their athletic performance. The team called this group (over fifteen million people) the "change seekers." The last group, the "active lifestyle consumers," represented some of the thirty-five million people with active lives and special nutritional concerns. In the meeting, they developed a three-tiered pyramid that guided the strategy for the next three years. Each layer represented a segment of customers; each segment was associated with its key channel of distribution;

and each segment received a unique sub-brand (HP/High Performance, Myoplex, and AdvantEdge, for instance), a unique product line of supplements, and a unique set of endorsers, ranging from Shannon Sharpe to Christie Brinkley.

For each tier, the management group looked at the market and identified clear holes that they could enter immediately. For instance, at the top end, there was the opportunity for turning powdered supplements into a range of ready-to-drink meal replacements. At the lower end of the pyramid, there was room for a product that fit between diet products like Ultra Slim-Fast and geriatric products like Boost. This new line was introduced in Wal-Mart stores. While working on this line, the management team rebuilt the supply chain of vendors to meet the speed and cost requirements of large, new EAS customers like Wal-Mart. They rationalized and developed new partnerships with fewer manufacturers of EAS product. This rebuilding was possible at the same time that they were expanding the product line, because the fundamental ingredients were similar, differing primarily in mix, packaging, and performance levels. The results were like a sprinter exploding off the blocks from a standing start. In 2001, sales increased almost instantly from $157 million to $217 million. In 2002, they increased yet again, to $270 million, all while the company expanded margins and increased its reinvestment rate.

Central to the new strategy was building on the core of science and zealot users, with high retention rates year to year and an extremely high rate of willingness to buy the new products. This recognition of the core mission permeates the culture of the company. As Dave Lumley says, "If you can get people to think beyond worrying about market share in Cincinnati and worry about the core of the company, you are on the way."[11] While the expansion required entering new channels, like Wal-Mart, each initiative was less than two steps away from this core because of shared formulations, brand, science, infrastructure, and competitors. The team conducted extensive market research and targeted gaps in the market and a large, expanding profit pool. Supplements and health drinks are among the highest-margin consumable items in a $10 billion market that is expected to exceed $15 billion by 2007. Finally, the new products were targeted at openings in the market for which leadership economics were possible. EAS is the leader both in direct meal replacements and supplements, with 28 percent share, and in specialty-store meal replacements and supplements, with about 20 percent share, and has rapidly broken into the top three in the mass channel share. It is now the fastest-growing active lifestyle nutrition brand. The speed with which EAS restarted its growth engine is a testament to the ability of the new management team to create direction and energy, as well as to the power of the key adjacency principles of profit pool targeting, insistence on leadership economics, and protection and projection of the strong core.

The Defensive Side of Adjacencies

Sometimes an adjacency move is dictated by a competitor's threat. Occasionally, such a threat demands only monitoring; other times, it requires immediate action.

Eastman Kodak Company traces its core product line of film, developing materials, and cameras back to 1879, when George Eastman filed for his first patent, a method to make dry gelatin plates for cameras—a method that he had developed in his mother's kitchen at the age of twenty-four. In 1884, he devised a way of capturing images on film and wrote in a letter, "I believe in the future of the film business."[12] By 1888, he had added cameras to the product line and named them Kodak, a synthetic name starting with the first letter of Kilbourn, his mother's family name. One of his early customers, the warden of the Illinois State Penitentiary, wrote to him about the use of the camera in mug shots to track criminals or to circulate images of those who escaped. From that early start until one hundred years later, in 1990, Kodak grew to dominate its segment, with over 80 percent U.S. market share in film and developing agents, nearly 50 percent of processing, and a product line mirroring the original three areas of George Eastman. But then things began to change. Competitors along virtually every expansion vector changed, putting Kodak on the defensive around its total perimeter (figure 3-2).

The first competitor was Fuji, entering the U.S. market for film in 1984 with lower prices, the aggressive sponsorship of the Olympics, and the defiant act of floating its blimp over Kodak's headquarters in Rochester, New York. Fuji gained market share from zero to 18 percent in 1997, when it further dropped prices at the low end of the market—attack vector one. Kodak has matched prices and launched a two-tiered film strategy. At the same time, 1997 was the year that digital cameras began to noticeably take off, led by Sony. Kodak has made digital camera technology its top R&D

FIGURE 3 - 2

Kodak's Competitive Adjacency Challenge

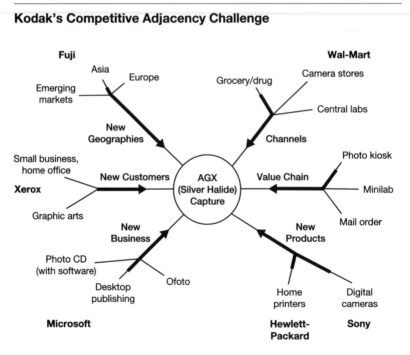

Note: Thick arrows indicate threats.

priority, and has captured the number two camera position, but does not yet make money in digital products—attack vector two.

A third vector affecting Kodak's market dynamics from yet another adjacency is in film processing and photofinishing. Wal-Mart's growth, control, and leadership in traditional film processing has formed a much stronger counterpoint to Kodak's leadership than ever before. On top of Wal-Mart's growth are the Internet-based processing businesses like Shutterfly and PhotoPoint for the transfer of digital pictures to paper. Again, Kodak has invested resources to match this adjacency, heroically creating the most visited Web photo site and buying online processor Ofoto—attack vector number four. Vector five, in a seemingly dizzying blitz from home printers, in which Hewlett-Packard is the leader with 70 percent market share, allowed consumers to print their own digital photos at home, not necessarily using Kodak paper. In response, Kodak introduced an ink-jet printer, the Personal Picture Maker, manufactured by Lexmark. Yet another vector, the sixth, is in PC software, especially Microsoft Windows, which has an embedded subroutine to link users with Web sites favored by Microsoft. This adjacency logic could be extended even further to small-business graphics with Xerox and to the makers of small, self-contained development mini-labs where new, high-tech competitors are starting to make inroads on a related Kodak processing equipment business.

In one sense, market opportunities for Kodak abound. There are new products, more widespread use of imagery, and much more direct customer contact in Internet sales than ever before. On the other hand, these simultaneous vectors make Kodak's strategic challenge seem like a *Star Wars* video game, with threats coming from every attack angle through all the adjacencies to its core business.

Common Pitfalls in the Evaluation of Adjacencies

Businesses can use the approaches outlined in this chapter to look at all three investments of offensive moves, defensive moves and threats, and hedges against distant developments. Several pitfalls in accurately evaluating growth opportunities were highlighted repeatedly by the CEO interviews and our interpretations of the paired comparison stories. A more rigorous decision process can help a business executive avoid these and other common pitfalls:

- Mistaking a large market for a large profit pool

- Failing to understand how tightly the profit pool is controlled by a competitor

- Misunderstanding the root cause of market power, thereby defining leadership in the wrong way

- Underestimating how today's competitive dynamics will shift tomorrow's profit pool

- Not doing adequate homework on relative cost position across competitors, thereby underestimating the true economic strength of the leader

- Falling prey to the tyranny of incremental economics and, in so doing, dismissing the importance of leadership economics in reinvestment

Overarching these specific areas of potential failures of decision making is what I term the tyranny of the apparent strategic rationale. In certain situations, there is enormous pressure to act, even if the numbers do not add up. For example, when a competitor moves into an adjacency, a company feels pressure to follow, or to fail. An extreme example of this is the purchase of wireless licenses by British Telecom, Deutsche Telekom, and France Telecom. Each company felt compelled to rush into these expensive investments, in auction, with no clear leadership strategy in mind. The purchase by each put these three providers of phone services in Europe into massive debt and financial stress that eventually resulted in the resale of these same licenses at a huge loss. Competitive moves are tough not to copy in the heat of battle. Nevertheless, some of the most costly errors have come from lemming-like competitor behaviors.

Untested assumptions about customer buying preferences are the other source of siren songs, which have led many companies into massive and costly adjacency moves that they have subsequently had to unravel. The most common arena in which businesses rely on untested assumptions is financial services, and the most common topic is customer bundling. The belief in the concept of a financial supermarket has led companies like American Express (in the mid-1980s) into a range of product adjacencies that turned out to be costly, far from their true cores, and unjustified by customer interest. This rationale has appeared in other industries, too, such as in consulting, where the disastrous strategy of Saatchi & Saatchi, a U.K. consulting firm begun in the 1980s, was unraveled at great cost in the following decade. In the travel industry, Allegis used this kind of untested logic and assembled an airline (United Airlines), a rental car company (Hertz), and a hotel chain (Sheraton), believing that an integrated set of travel products would be well received by corporate customers. They weren't.

Assumptions about customer bundling or competitor mimicry are often so powerful that they compel management teams to forgo the usual analysis and concept testing. This has proved to be a dangerous route.

The Surprising Sophistication of Simplicity

Deciding on economic criteria is the starting point in choosing an adjacency opportunity, and there is a wide range of criteria. If the management team fails to agree on these criteria, it may reach a decision inefficiently or may even reach the wrong decision. Few teams spend enough time clarifying the absolute requirements, and those that can be waived, in a portfolio of investments in growth that might have quite different objectives and risk profiles.

Throughout my study of how companies evaluate growth and how their CEOs think about the ultimate decisions, I was struck by the seeming paradox that the best companies had a few simple criteria that everyone understood and agreed to. Furthermore, the most thorough evaluations proved to be most important in the areas highlighted by the paired comparisons: robustness of the profit pool, the ability to be differentiated and achieve leadership-level economics, and the ability to manage risk that comes through real relatedness to a strong core. The power of establishing clear, simple, rigorous criteria (and what can happen when this was not done) is shown in the history of Lloyds Bank under Sir Brian Pitman.

As his comments in the following paragraphs indicate, Lloyds's transformation really began in earnest when Pitman took over and established a primary focus of a single measure, return on capital relative to the cost of capital, which drove the company's divestitures and investments for over a decade. This singular focus provides a powerful lesson. What is especially important, though, is to understand the rigor that went into the calculation of this central number. In every major adjacency decision, the key inputs were the three just highlighted—the ability to be differentiated and achieve leadership economics, the robustness of the profit pool, and the relatedness to a strong core. The rest of this chapter will describe the importance of these inputs in the criteria that Lloyds Bank applied to the adjacencies it avoided, such as investment banking; the adjacencies it exited, such as California banking; and the adjacencies the company entered, such as the mortgage business. Pitman describes some of these decisions in detail:

> When I took over we had extremely woolly objectives. We were going to be good to shareholders, and employees, and everyone under the sun. Instead, I wanted a single, governing objective—a driving force by which we could measure our success. We had an excellent board and, at a board meeting shortly after my appointment, we had a debate on what constituted success for Lloyds Bank—and we could not agree! Yet, we realized we had to agree on what we were trying to

accomplish before we could measure our performance. There seemed to be an obsession with becoming the biggest, or at least the biggest in the U.K. Some believed in a target of 50 percent outside of the U.K. Some felt all that mattered was customer satisfaction.

I argued that our shares were selling below net asset value. Our return on equity was inadequate. That should be our sole driving force. Ultimately, the board, with some reluctance, agreed. The interesting thing is that these arguments about definitions of success still hold true today. For example, many companies pay lip service to shareholder value but their real driving force is to get bigger. At Lloyds Bank, originally we set ourselves a target of 10 percent above the 5 percent rate of inflation, but revised it when we discovered our then cost of equity was an appalling 17 to 19 percent after tax. After a lot of argument, we compromised on 18 percent. This choice of governing objective and target proved to be a tremendous driving force.

The first thing we lighted on was Lloyds Bank, California, [which was] earning 8 percent ROE. We bought it in 1974 to diversify away from the U.K. It was earning 8 percent because we were a minnow in this market. It was a growth market, but no one had looked hard at whether we had competitive advantage. Withdrawing was like pulling teeth. This was one of the fastest-growing economies in the world. How could we withdraw? I asked when it would have a positive net present value, and no one could prove it would ever have one. So, we sold the bank for a handsome price, and lo and behold, share price went up and the cost of equity went down.[13]

"The market economics and our weak competitive position against the major players persuaded us that we should not follow competitors that were moving into investment banking in the Big Bang of 1988," says Pitman. "If we are looking at things we didn't do, that was probably the most important decision we made. Against the big U.S. investment banks in particular, we could see no competitive advantage on which we could build. No one could tell me how we would compete or when we would earn our cost of capital. So we shut down our small operation."

After a series of divestitures, Lloyds began its rebuilding program around its branch network. Using these same strict economic criteria, Lloyds began investing in its distribution system and acquiring product lines that could be sold in the branches, including the acquisition of Abbey Life for its life insurance product and the acquisition of Cheltenham & Gloucester, a leading mortgage provider. Pitman says that about this time, he looked to an unexpected model for his performance criteria:

> [I] came up with a new performance measure, which was the time to double the value of your company. At a meeting, Coca-Cola suggested that if you wanted to be world class in value creation you had to double shareholder value every three years. Some contended that comparing ourselves to a soft drinks company was wrong because banks were in more competitive markets. I said, "I think we can; why not?" I had a study done and found that banks were way down the list of market competitiveness and that soft drinks were close to the top. And we were able to double our value every three years for seventeen years. Everything we looked at was compared on the dimension of value creation. This is what kept us with our core business, and this is what pushed us far ahead of our competition.
>
> What are the three main lessons from my career? One of the major lessons is to have this debate on what constitutes success. The debate about what is success is crucial. It is not easy to get agreement on this, but agreeing on a single governing objective and a method of measuring it helps to focus resources. Everything else becomes a means to that end. The second thing, highly related to the first, is really to understand this question of competitive advantage. How do you build and sustain it? The third thing is that, in today's environment, only the most productive companies are going to win.

So, what are the practical lessons learned from looking at adjacency strategies with a wide range of outcomes, at companies with different success rates, and at the criteria used by those companies as described by the CEOs making the decisions?

This chapter has uncovered a number of lessons:

- Don't assume that you have consensus on the decision criteria and the decision process. Even some of the most established companies can drift.

- Establish a small number of economic criteria, maybe even one, into which the key assumptions all funnel. Communicate it over and over.

- Consider whether a focused, off-site meeting could force more rigorous and consistent evaluation of adjacency moves. Develop a common vocabulary and method to look at the full portfolio of past moves and future opportunities. Without such a process, how will decisions be made?

- Ensure that the three key drivers of adjacency potential—potential leadership economics, relatedness to a strong core, and a robust profit pool—are front and center. If not, understand why.

- Avoid the grand strategic rationale.

- Use the same criteria (even with different hurdle rates) to evaluate new investments as well as exits and adjacencies of all types.

4

Orchestrating Adjacency Moves

Strengthening the Core
Versus Investing in Adjacencies

Up until now we have said relatively little about the condition of the core business itself. Yet, it is the central character in all dramas concerning adjacency moves. Even the most attractive growth opportunity can turn unattractive, unrealistic, or even destructive when bolted onto the wrong core business, or onto the right business at the wrong time. And even a relatively modest adjacency move by a strong core business with pent-up resources to invest can act as a catalyst to trigger a burst of new growth. Indeed, we found that more than 80 percent of the most successful companies achieved a large portion of their profitable growth by moving into adjacencies surrounding their original core business.

The importance of the "state of the core" is apparent in the contrast of Carter's and UPS. Carter's, the leading maker of sleeper clothing for babies, made adjacency moves in the 1980s into retail and into totally new customer segments. The problem was that the business was in disarray and these otherwise sensible moves served only to magnify the burden placed on an overtaxed core. By contrast,

UPS's modest $70 million move into the service parts logistics business quickly unleashed a series of actions that resulted in a $1 billion leadership business just a few years later. The timing was totally wrong for Carter's and perfect for UPS. This chapter focuses on this critical judgment regarding the state of the core.

Core businesses differ widely in their abilities to support a major new growth initiative. The three critical dimensions along which they vary are competitive position, market dynamics, and financial performance (figure 4-1). Competitive position can range all the way from a weak follower to a strong market leader with parity or weak leadership common in intermediate situations. Market dynamics range from strong growth to stable low growth to total meltdown. Financial performance can vary from full potential to underperformance. Ironically, the businesses with the strongest competitive positions and the highest economic returns also tend to be the most prone to performance below their full potential. This paradoxical conclusion stems from the ability of a leading business to achieve strong earnings while underperforming, the internal dynamics that allow the best businesses more latitude in budget

FIGURE 4 - 1

Critical Dimensions of Core Situations

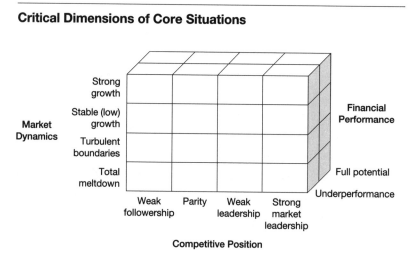

and target setting, and the ample opportunities available for the best businesses. By contrast, businesses with weak competitive positions are preoccupied with survival and typically are not surrounded by an abundance of high-quality opportunities.

My earlier book, *Profit from the Core,* established the strong link between sustained, profitable growth and leadership in a highly focused core business. Specifically, 88 percent of the sustained-value-creating companies had strong leadership in one or two core businesses, and 80 percent of these companies aggressively used adjacency expansions to fuel their growth. In our interviews with CEOs running companies with dominant and focused core businesses, it became apparent that these companies had much-higher-than-average success rates in moving successfully into adjacencies. One of the important elements of their success, of course, is the strength of the core business that they were using as their platform for new growth.

Importance of Determining the State of the Core

It is critical to understand exactly how your core business is positioned along the dimensions in this simple matrix depicted in the figure. The placement may not be as obvious as it might seem on the surface. Understanding competitive position means defining the relevant market boundaries precisely. Is Xerox in the xerography business or the document creation business? Is Coke in the cola business, the soft drinks business, or the beverage business? Which arena is most important? Dell's competitive stranglehold over the personal computer business was virtually absolute well before the company attained the largest market share. Industry leadership stems from market power and influence, from low-cost economics, and from control over the industry profit pool. These are only partly related to scale, which is often a secondary factor in the equation. So, these determinations about true competitive position are not the easiest of judgments and are prone to distortion.

Determining whether a business is performing at its full potential or far below it can also be difficult. Of two hundred executives surveyed, half believed that their strongest core business was not close to, probably not even within 50 percent of, its true potential for profitable growth. But which of them were right? Arguably, Anheuser-Busch's costly foray away from beer and into the snack food business (Eagle Snacks, Earthgrain Bread, etc.) was driven by an underestimate of the further profit and growth potential in its core beer business. It is interesting that the subsequent exit from these troubled snack businesses was followed by a burst of new growth and profits in the beer business, suddenly the recipient of full management attention again.

Most companies participate in many businesses, though one or two dominant cores usually deliver the true economic profit. These strong cores are often surrounded by weaker positions that have their own adjacency opportunities. If you have a portfolio of businesses, it is critical to have a common framework like the axes of figure 4-1 and a clear point of view on the relative position of each of the different cores. The odds of adjacency success vary so much by position in the matrix that this should be a precondition of decisions to fund new growth initiatives. For instance, we examined the data used earlier on 181 adjacency moves in the United States and the United Kingdom. The average success rate across the whole sample was 27 percent. Doing this same analysis for those companies that were clear leaders and those that were followers or at parity revealed that the odds of success were nearly three times higher for the company starting with a leadership position than for a weak follower.

On the following pages, I examine the evidence and provide ideas to make these judgments. I focus primarily on three situations: (1) a weak, or longtime follower, business, (2) a business whose core market is declining rapidly—the melting-core situation, and (3) a business with clear leadership of a market or niche, where the core is suspected not to be performing at its full economic potential.

The Harsh Reality of the Weak Follower

The world is filled with companies that are distant followers in their industry. Some may contain a small core of strength buried among weaker positions. Others may no longer have a viable core in which competitive advantage remains. These companies are dying to leap to a new lily pad, fleeing their core. These are companies like Budget Rent A Car, a distant follower purchased and sold six times, mostly to financial buyers or people not in the rental business, who believed they were going to be the ones to unlock the value. Budget made adjacency moves into travel businesses and even purchased Ryder. All was for naught, and the company has finally been purchased by Cendant, which will combine Budget with its strong Avis division. Integration into a leader is the most attractive final home for most distant followers. Alternatively, among the distant followers are companies like Chrysler, which is a perpetual follower in the auto business and which was able to regroup around a strong core buried deep within layers of weaker products and segments. So, what are the real odds that adjacency moves will reposition a company, springing it free from the bonds of followership?

My team found that surprisingly few studies have been conducted on the odds of a longtime industry follower's achieving market leadership position or economic returns equivalent to the leader's. One English study of manufacturing companies in the 1980s found the odds that a follower will move from position number four and below into the top two spots over ten years was only 12 percent.[1] Another survey of several studies found that the odds were even lower.[2] Jim Collins, in his book *Good to Great,* identified only eleven out of all 1,435 companies that appeared on the *Fortune* 500 list from 1965 to 1995 that had moved from economic stagnancy to outperforming the stock market by a factor of three or more over a fifteen-year period. All of the eleven companies had, somewhere within the organization, a strong core position, albeit an underperforming one, that new management was able to capitalize upon. They were not followers that turned around, but companies sitting on some fundamentally strong assets that had been under-performing and that could be stabilized and then expanded into new adjacencies.

Though no longer maintained actively, the PIMS database is one of the few longitudinal sources of empirical data on the competitive positions of three thousand businesses over time. I was able to tap into this source of information by working with MANTIS/Empirametrics, a company that has built a model based on these extensive historical relationships. The model can simulate changes in competitive positions over time. I worked with MANTIS to analyze the frequency with which followers make large gains. We looked at companies that were number four in their industry, half the size of the number three competitor. On average, only 7 percent of one thousand randomly generated simulations under all kinds of conditions resulted in a doubling of these followers' low market share over a five-year period. Seventy-two percent of them lost ground from an already weak position; some drifted into oblivion.

Only under two sets of conditions would a distant follower move up significantly. In the first situation, the follower was able to suddenly come up with a unique product advantage in its core relative to the leader (see the EMC example below). In the second condition, the follower developed a successful strategy directly targeting an equally weak follower, confiscating its share, but not chipping away at the leader. Again, the feasibility of this strategy is low. Movement to a totally new adjacency did not even come up as a viable alternative. These findings, based on a database that was once a legend in the annals of business analysis, embedded in MANTIS's simulation model, reinforced the findings about the low odds and selected success patterns for distant followers to pursue.

To further understand the potential for adjacency moves to bail out companies in follower positions, my team looked at fifty-one industries and 501 companies over ten years. We chose industries for which consistent market share data were available (not easy to do, it turns out) and whose competitors could be isolated for examination. We found that leadership is quite sticky over ten years and that the companies in the top two spots were displaced only 29 percent of the time over the same period. Of the 399 companies in positions number three through number ten, the odds of attaining status in the top two were 12 percent for companies starting in positions number three through number five and were only 8 percent for those starting farther back. A parallel multiyear performance analysis of 494 companies in fifty industry sectors in Japan found similar results on the difficulty of dramatically shifting strategic position. Just under 12 percent of followers in positions number three through number ten moved into a number one or number two position, and just 5 percent of those companies did so from number six or below over, in general, a ten-year period traced for each. More importantly, for the purpose of this book on adjacency expansions, relatively few of those companies that did move up and did create value by the end of the period did so using adjacency expansions, and *virtually none* did so with a major adjacency jump to a new position away from the core business.

The primary way (45 percent) that followers moved up the rankings in competitive position and financial performance was through industry consolidation, the merger or acquisition of direct industry competitors. An example is U.S. Foodservice (USF). Sara Lee spun off USF in 1989 as a leveraged buyout (LBO) with number six position in the United States and number three in its principal regional Midwest and Northeast markets. USF gradually built up stronger regional market share and then did a series of equity offerings, which enabled it to make seventeen acquisitions of similar businesses over a six-year period. The focus was always on improved operations; the introduction of proprietary, higher-margin private-label and signature brands; and the rapid integration of back-office activities into the core. From $890 million in revenues and $26 million in operating profit in 1989, USF grew to $6.9 billion in revenues and $250 million in operating earnings when Royal Ahold purchased it in 2000. Though the odds of executing a successful consolidation or roll-up strategy are less than 40 percent, such a strategy can be a powerful way to create leadership position and economics. A consolidation or roll-up strategy has four critical requirements: a stable platform to bolt acquisitions onto, a method to achieve real economies of scale, realistic acquisition pricing, and superb execution of the integration plan.

Shrink to Grow

Another way that distant followers bootstrapped themselves into leadership (20 percent of cases) was by redefining and building on a narrow customer segment, in which deep loyalty could be built through a uniquely tailored strategy. Dominance of a focused segment could then be a platform for further expansion. In a sense, this strategic retrenchment is a "shrink to grow" strategy.

MBNA is one successful example of this type of strategy. MBNA was started in 1982 as the credit card subsidiary of a regional savings bank called Maryland National. This bank had a weak and eroding competitive position that did not allow it to survive the real estate loan crisis that many banks encountered during the late 1980s. The distressed parent was acquired by what is now Bank of America, and the MBNA division was spun off as an independent public company. Its secret was segmentation of the credit card customer base by profession and affinity group, with a strategy to focus on the customers with the best economics and with the greatest potential for loyalty.[3] MBNA found that the best way to reach these customers was through affinity groups like universities and the National Education Association. This practice of pursuing affinity groups went back to the company's first core customer in 1982, the Alumni Association of Georgetown. Though other competitors issued these affinity-group credit cards, MBNA had a lead in know-how regarding customer segmentation and in servicing these groups to ensure their retention. Today MBNA is the third largest credit card issuer. From 1991 to 2000, it grew from $1.3 billion to $7.9 billion in revenues, and from $149 million to $1.3 billion in profit. And its success all stems back to the situation in which a focused niche business, buried inside a weak follower, becomes the new core and then expands aggressively into new customer adjacencies and highly targeted payment vehicles for each.

A further method that lagging companies sometimes used to make gains was the dramatic revamping of a core product line that had lost its edge. This strategy accounted for only 10 percent of turnarounds in competitive position. Perhaps the best illustration of this form of turnaround since the mid-1990s is EMC, a company that ended the year 2000 having provided its shareholders with a 69 percent compound annual rate of return over the previous ten years.

In 1988, EMC had $120 million in revenues, but was losing $30 million in profit and was in the throes of a major product quality crisis. Defective disk drives in its core storage products were losing customer files, and the product line was proving to be too broad for a company of its size to support technically and extend scientifically. Mike Ruettgers, hired in 1988 as executive vice president of operations, organized to fix the core quality problem. After being promoted to president in 1989, he then attacked the strategy issue. In what turned out to be a brilliant and counterintuitive choice, he exited nine major product lines constituting 80 percent of EMC's revenues in order to bet the company on a single product initiative. His attack plan seems even bolder when you consider that it targeted IBM's storage products for IBM's own mainframes, in which EMC's target had more than 75 percent market share.

EMC's key insight was that the IBM storage devices were nearly ten times larger than they needed to be as well as being expensive and slow. By moving away from IBM's architecture of large, complex single disk drives to dozens of small drives like those in personal computers, the company achieved its product breakthrough. Three years later, EMC had evolved from a weak follower to the leading supplier of storage for IBM's own mainframes. From there EMC used the same concept to expand into a common storage platform that could be used with any type of computer, not just IBM's. Today EMC is the leader in high-end storage systems, with 40 percent worldwide share and a strong joint venture with Dell. By contrast, IBM is number two, with 22 percent share of the market. The years 2001 and 2002 have seen a slump in the market for large systems, and pricing for storage devices has collapsed. Every participant in the industry, including EMC, has experienced lower sales. However, there is no denying EMC's design and execution of a shrink-to-grow strategy to leadership from a follower position.

Many factors constrain the options of a weak follower. For instance, weak followers have access to almost no capital to invest relative to the leader in most businesses. In an analysis of thirty-three industries and 185 companies studied in depth by Bain, where profit was calculated for all main competitors, almost the entire profit pool was captured by the top three competitors. Moreover, the stronger the leader, the more skewed the distribution of profits and value. The top two leaders had 40 percent of the revenues, on average, but 70 percent of the profits and 80 percent of the value and new growth. Furthermore, other studies of the drivers of company profitability consistently reveal competitive position to be much more important than market choice. We calculate that if your objective is new, profitable growth, it is at least three times better to have a very strong position in a lower-growth industry than a weak position in a hot industry.

Weak followers seldom find a miracle cure by jumping into an adjacent area, abandoning the follower core for a better position elsewhere. The odds of substantially improving a longtime position of weak followership are low. The three primary ways that have worked are not adjacency dependent. These options consist of combining with other competitors; finding the magic to create new, powerful product differentiation (as mentioned earlier, this is easier said than done); or retreating to build around a hidden core, an area of strength buried in a larger business.

Balancing the Core and Adjacencies in the Chrysler Turnaround

Chrysler had always been a follower. The company was founded in 1925 by Walter Percy Chrysler, a former General Motors executive, and quickly grew to become the fifth largest auto company in 1927, when it sold 192,000 cars. Chrysler stayed in the top five for the next seventy years until its acquisition by Daimler-Benz in 1998, once even briefly moving up to number two in the 1930s. Coincidentally, its acquirer was founded within less than one year of the birthday of Chrysler, in 1926. Benz had the earliest lineage of all, 1883, when Karl Benz founded his company Benz & Company in Mannheim, Germany. Gottlieb Daimler registered his *Reitwagen* ("riding carriage") with a "gas or petroleum engine" in 1885 and drove his first car, which had three wheels and a top speed of ten miles per hour, the following year in Stuttgart. The two companies were combined in 1926.

From 1952 to 1998, Chrysler had no fewer than eight major crises that brought the company to the brink of bankruptcy. In a 1993 speech to his four hundred key managers shortly after taking over as chairman and CEO, Bob Eaton said, "We have got to quit getting sick. I want to be the first chairman in the history of Chrysler not to have to lead the company back from the brink of bankruptcy."[4] He got his wish, though not with the ending he anticipated. When Chrysler was taken over it had record profits, 17 percent U.S. market share, a paid-up pension fund balance for the first time since 1957, and $7 billion in cash in the bank. Sales reached $61.4 billion in 1996, more than double the level of 1991. The long prosperity and low gasoline prices of the mid- to late 1990s had created a huge demand for large vehicles, and Chrysler was producing hot models in each of the hottest segments: the Dodge Ram pickup truck, the Town & Country minivan, and several sport utility vehicles such as the Jeep Grand Cherokee and the Dodge Durango.

The complexity of the auto industry is immense, and histories of each car company and the overall business fill whole sections of business libraries. Chrysler, the perpetual follower, but also the perpetual survivor, does illustrate many of the points made in this book about followership and expansion beyond the core. Perhaps the most telling example is how the company faced its greatest crisis in 1980, when the U.S. government loaned Chrysler $1.5 billion to keep it solvent in the midst of three years of losses totaling $2.5 billion, including a whopping $1.8 billion loss in 1980, the largest loss ever for a U.S. company. But how did it dig itself out of this hole from such weak followership?

Our interviews with people who were there at the time highlighted three key elements. As Hal Sperlich, the much-celebrated product designer at the center of such hits as the Mustang and the Chrysler minivan, explains, the first element was the identification of the true core of Chrysler, and the consolidation around that core to grow:

"When I arrived at Chrysler from Ford, there was not much at the end of the 1970s to build on that was strongly competitive. Chrysler was selling cars, but that was about it. What strength did they have that could constitute a core? They had the compact segment, the Aspen and Volare models, targeting a market of working people with modest incomes. But we did find something to work with. We had America's first front-wheel-drive car. This provided a huge fundamental advantage in manufacturing cost, design flexibility, and fuel efficiency, if we could take advantage of it. We had this terrific little nugget of power train that was geared up for front wheel drive and one customer segment who would buy our cars. Our first product from this base was the K cars, America's first front-wheel-drive compact car to replace the Volare and the Aspen. This was the first common platform car outside of Japan which produced a new core to build adjacencies off of that platform."[5]

The second requirement was to simplify the core, reducing costs and grinding out efficiency to produce some form of new growth initiative. Central to this was complexity reduction: a decrease in the number of models, the layers of management, and the number of component suppliers. The actions taken then have rippled through to today, probably allowing the company to survive—a lesson many followers might heed. For instance, the use of outsourced components became religion. By the late 1990s, Chrysler outsourced 70 percent of its components compared with 50 percent for Ford and only 30 percent for General Motors. The number of suppliers declined from three thousand in 1980 to one thousand in 1990 to 650 in 1995. The automaker also reduced product complexity:

"We calculated that we had fifty million permutations in each car line in 1980 and took it down to as low as 2,500. This forced the marketing group to know their market and find out what would sell. You just can't expect the dealer to do this. It made manufacturing and sourcing much more efficient. It was a pretty powerful tool, massively increasing product velocity through the pipeline. This created a totally different picture than when I arrived and found thousands of cars in the fairgrounds sitting in the mud, having been built to inventory. At the same time that Honda was implementing demand pull so successfully that consumers were waiting in the parking lot for the trailer to pull up [so that they could] drive the car away directly. The bottom line is that we were resource constrained and we simply had to cut cost. The result was to take out nearly 10 percent of the total systems cost of a vehicle and one-third of variable product cost, which liberated critical resources to refresh the product line and also increased quality at the same time."[6]

The third key ingredient in Chrysler's turnaround was the discovery of an adjacency expansion off of the core to fuel growth and reposition the company. This had a measure of luck, but an even larger measure of brilliance. The adjacency expansion included both the invention of the minivan with front wheel drive and the purchase of American Motors to get Jeep, a huge, underperforming franchise. Together, these moves repositioned Chrysler away from passenger cars, in which it was a weak follower, maybe hopelessly, into a new space where it could have some leadership economics. For the fifteen years from 1980 to 1995, minivans and SUVs accounted for more than 100 percent of the profit made by the company from selling vehicles. Sperlich elaborates:

"By the time we had done the minivan, we had gotten rid of all of the products in the original core and were in the process of redefining the business, even redefining what cars were, through our focus on front wheel drive, the launch of the minivan, and the use of platform cars. The minivan created a new segment between cars and station wagons. It had all of what Lee Iacocca and I would call the "killer ABCs" of marketing. In this case they were fuel efficiency, family-sized maximum utility, and friendly prices, pretty powerful selling points taken together."

The success of the Chrysler turnaround, interestingly, did lead to the desire for adjacency expansion far from the core, a move that we have seen over and over again throughout this book. Chrysler went into the car rental business, purchasing a virtual menagerie of Dollar, General, Snappy, and Thrifty (all money losers by 1990). It also purchased Gulfstream Aerospace and an electronics company, putting them into a holding company structure in 1997. All have since been divested. Lee Iaccoca, who led the diversification, later said of these large investments: "We wasted a lot of time, a lot of effort, setting up a holding company. I was never a conglomerate type of thinker anyway."[7]

In 1992, two years before these investments were made, a review of twenty years in the auto industry confirmed the importance of sticking to the core: "The lessons seem clear. The automakers did well when they concentrated on their core businesses, wrung inefficiencies out of operations, and gave their employees clear direction. They faltered when they diversified out of their core, neglected day to day activities, and sent mixed signals to managers with grandiose but botched reorganizations."[8]

Every industry is different. The auto industry is a world unto itself. However, the lessons of business economics penetrate here too with regard to the requirements and elements of followership success, survival, and, usually in the end, ultimate combinations with others.

The Dreaded Melting Core

The challenge of managing a business whose entire core product market is eroding inexorably is not common. At any point in time, our analysis shows that only about 2 to 3 percent of markets are in severe secular decline. Fortunately, our analysis also shows that most of the cases are of longer-term erosion that management would have seen coming, rather than a sudden, dramatic, surprising disappearance of demand. Some historical examples would include companies that mined coal in industrial countries that began restricting its use, companies that made polyester fiber for clothing when consumers switched back to cotton, and manufacturers of vinyl for use in phonograph records. In searching our database for melting cores, we have identified two approaches that sometimes provided a way out of this extremely troublesome dilemma. Both involved adjacency expansion combined with systematic thinking and hard work—there were no miracle cures here.

Imation: Escape from the Melting Core

A movie fittingly called *The Core* was released as I was writing this chapter. *The Core* was about a crisis facing planet earth with the erosion of the earth's core. The movie's tag line was "The only way out is first to go in." It seems to capture well the way that Imation has dealt with its own melting core. Look up 3M's financial performance, and you will see an almost unbroken, upward trajectory of stock price through good economies and bad, from $3 in 1970 to $130 in 2002, a remarkably steady profile of 12.4 percent growth in value per year. The secret is partly 3M's continuous ability to come up with new and innovative products from its core technology. From *In Search of Excellence* (published in the early 1980s) to the more recent *Built to Last,* business books on the most successful companies have celebrated this ability. Another method has been the company's actions to spin off or sell businesses that it felt were about to encounter much slower-growth and lower-margin market conditions. The company's primary move on this dimension was the creation of Imation in July 1996 as a spin-off of seven businesses to the public. For its first years, Imation's stock price was flat until January 2001, but has since nearly tripled along with the financial prospects.

Imation's CEO, Bill Monahan, has become an expert at mining growth from tough positions. He changed nine out of ten people in the top management and developed a strategic focus of trying to "create proprietary niches off of our core technologies." Imation has become especially expert at working with partners on complex product extensions that blend several technologies. Today, Monahan explains, nearly 100 percent of the company's major product launches and development projects have one or more partners: "This is highly contentious and very tough to do by its very nature. The ability to set up joint venture partnerships that work is a core skill in our company, has taken a long time to develop, and is now the primary engine for our expansion into new products and adjacencies."[9]

One of Imation's long-term products has captured a leading position in floppy disks, a removable, magnetic storage medium for personal computers. The good news is that this is a leadership and profitable position. The bad news is that the market for floppy disk drives has been heading for inexorable decline since 1992 at an astonishing rate of 19 percent per year, being replaced by optical storage. Talk about a melting core! Imation does not have optical manufacturing capabilities, but it does possess several more enduring and fungible assets such as the leading brand name in storage, optical technology, customer relationships, and a worldwide distribution infrastructure. So, it has identified a rapidly growing, large-scale, high-quality manufacturer of optical storage media with the best cost economics in the world and developed a joint arrangement to attack the worldwide market using Imation's infrastructure. This is a win-win for both parties, as Imation gets access to quality products at low cost while its partner gains access to worldwide markets, increases its share and scale, and further improves its operating results. Imation has further enhanced its profitability by targeting the more profitable business segments of the market. As Monahan says, "In some ways this is more than an adjacency expansion; it will ultimately become a total replacement of a major piece of our core and possibly our largest core business."

On the surface, Imation's expansion strategy sounds straightforward, but it is anything but that. Just think of the many companies that failed to take assets like distribution and brand when the core product was eroding and leverage them to obtain a new lease on life. One example is Polaroid, the instant-photography leader that announced bankruptcy in 2002. Polaroid had arguably one of the best brand names, deep knowledge of customer use of instant imaging, a knowledge of lenses, the ability to make camera housings, and so on. Yet, the company never made the jump to digital products, allowing instead these once-valuable infrastructure assets to lose value, to their eventual demise.

Think of the melting-core businesses you have experienced as a consumer and what became of the leader. What happened to IBM's typewriter business? What became of Gestetner, the leader in mimeograph machines? Or Northland, the leader in wooden skis? What about Wang, the leader in minicomputers? Some businesses, such as Northland and Gestetner, no longer exist, whereas others have used adjacency expansions to try to leverage their remaining strengths.

The other way to play the infrastructure card is to attempt to leverage a strong but declining franchise in a major product into a services business. This changeover seldom happens successfully, as it begs the question of whether the services business can be made into something sustainable beyond just servicing the declining product. Occasionally, however, a strong but declining installed base of product has been leveraged into a successful services business that eventually redefines the core and offsets the market decline. Most of the best examples we could find are in computer equipment or software markets, whose product life cycles have proved to be short and fragile since the 1980s.

Among the success cases are Wang's move from a pioneering but declining position in minicomputers into information technology, network services, and consulting before being purchased by the Dutch company Getronics in 1999. Getronics, today a global information and communications services company, has roots going back to 1887. Originally an installer of control equipment for the utilities and shipbuilding industries, the company itself has shifted to services, which now constitute 71 percent of its business. With the acquisition of Wang, two companies, one now inside the other, play out the same commercial choreography in a turbulent market. Getronics has done this primarily through acquisition, purchasing twenty-nine service companies from 1990 to 2002.

The situation of the melting core may signal that it's time to combine with another company or that the core may assume new status in a multicore company, as an asset to manage for cash. However, before any strategy is identified as the preferred alternative, it is worth looking closely at the gambits used by Imation through its infrastructure, or by others in services. The odds of making these adjacency strategies successful are not extremely high, but are definitely worth exploring and even pressure-testing in the field if you are endowed with infrastructure to build upon.

The Underperforming (but Strong) Core

One of the most difficult judgments for a CEO of a business with a strong core, or a strong niche position, is determining whether the core is performing at full potential. This judgment will drive the decision about how to balance the tension between continuing to mine the core—perhaps denying all but a handful of adjacency bets (if any)—and driving aggressively out beyond the core.

AmBev: Choosing the Right Path

Consider the case of AmBev, the leading South American beer company and today one of the best performers among all Brazilian companies. AmBev was purchased in 1989 by a group of financial private investors, led by the present CEO, Marcel Telles. The company was not performing well relative to other companies in general, but was a coleader with Antarctica, another Brazilian beer, and was performing similarly. It would have been possible for the new owners to feel that the core was close to its full potential and to use the extensive distribution network of the company to launch into other product and segment adjacencies, leveraging this fixed asset to drive new incremental profits. But they did not take this pathway. Instead, they decided that the core business was not close to its full operating and profit potential and that focusing on rebuilding the platform from scratch would generate profits and be a launch pad for adjacencies in the future. They chose the right path. AmBev is now the leading brewer in South America and the fourth largest brewer in the world. In the twelve years from 1989 to 2001, AmBev grew from 700 million Brazilian reals in revenues to 6.5 billion reals, an annual growth rate of 20.4 percent in a low-growth market, fueling an annual growth rate of stock valuation of 34.4 percent.

Brahma was a hundred-year-old brand of beer, second in market share in Brazil, with about 45 percent of the market. A Swiss immigrant to Brazil had named the beer after an Eastern god; the brewer had wanted to re-create the dark, rich beer of his homeland. A century after its founding, the company that became the foundation of AmBev had experienced decades of near zero growth, had no strong culture, and was enduring aging equipment, razor-thin profit margins, and low productivity. Telles describes the situation:

> The growth story of AmBev actually began with ten years of cost cutting and cultural rebuilding in the core business. This takes time. We [eventually] instilled a culture . . . of being intensely dissatisfied with anything less than full potential and results. We reinforced this with all sorts of systems, like our management room with a huge board that has on it every senior executive's business objectives, including mine, and progress against those objectives for all to see. We realized that we had bought a great market position, and discovered that we could constantly turn the screw more and more in the core business to extract much more than ever seemed [possible] at first glance. In 1989, AmBev had productivity of 1,200 hectoliters per employee. Today it has productivity of 8,200 hectoliters per employee, an increase of nearly seven times, and the improvements have come from virtually

everywhere. It is the power of these core economics that now
is allowing us to drive into new adjacencies successfully.[10]

The economic muscle that was built up in the core business
allowed AmBev to overtake and eventually simply wear down its
long-standing, more successful competitor, Antarctica. This led to a
merger between the two companies ten years later. The combination of Brahma and Antarctica, the company now called AmBev,
has captured 69 percent of the Brazilian beer market. This ten-year
run of productivity improvement and consolidation of its competitors allowed AmBev to drive its pretax profit margins from 8.7 percent to 30.5 percent. The robust cash flow source was used to invest
further in productivity and adjacency expansions from the core.
AmBev's timing could not have been better, given the growth in
beer consumption in Brazil. One study calculates that an amazing
42 percent of new growth in the world profit pool for beer will
come from Brazil.

In beer, AmBev drove its cost structure so low that it could move
into new markets outside Brazil and implant its operating system,
with lower prices than the incumbent in that country, yet with
higher profit margins and incentives to reinvest. Through this economic advantage, AmBev has now moved into adjacent geographic
areas in Uruguay and Paraguay, building to nearly 100 percent market share; into Argentina to reach 83 percent market share; into
Bolivia, attaining 99 percent share; and now into new beachhead
positions in Venezuela and Chile. This expansion strategy has made
AmBev the fourth largest and the most profitable brewer of beer in
the world, from an underperforming and marginally profitable
business that was the weaker of two market leaders in only one
country just twelve years earlier.

Today, AmBev is leveraging its distribution network of one million distribution points into further adjacencies in premium beer.
The company has driven the consumption of beer into new segments and "occasions" and has moved into soft drinks like the local
favorite, Guarana, made from a handpicked Amazonian berry, now
the second most popular drink after cola.

In concluding, Telles recounts the following story:

> The head of our beer university was a trained anthropologist who had once lived with the Aborigines in Australia. He learned two things there. One is that the Aborigines always said that they actually hunted the night before going out, for that is when they decided what they wanted and where they would go. Second was the power of focus. If they went hunting for lemur and another attractive animal like a kangaroo appeared, they would sometimes hear a hunter say, "It's easy; let's get that." But the leader always said, "We don't go after every animal that comes near us. You hunt the day before. Then you don't get distracted the day of the hunt. You don't go after the antelopes and the kangaroos if you are out hunting for lemur."

Achieving full potential in the core sometimes requires a major shock to the system as opposed to surgical interventions. At AmBev, management recognized the full potential gap right away and instituted a thorough program that affected the pay, roles, measurements, training, and incentives of every employee before turning to adjacency growth. At American Standard, described in the next section, Emmanuel Kampouris, the CEO at the time, recognized that there was the potential to drive asset utilization to a new level that could turn the company from near bankruptcy to stability and adjacency growth. The answer was an emergency retraining program that involved 22,000 employees in 110 factories. At GE Capital, the tremendous success of past acquisition-driven growth was becoming a less likely growth engine of the future, given the increased costs and scarcity of the right acquisition. The company recognized that it had unrealized potential in its core and embarked on a major program of training, tools, and measurement systems that it called Find, Win, Keep (FWK) and that later evolved to a program called Core Customer Connectivity (3C). The result was a booster rocket in its twenty-five operating units that fueled another wave of growth in the core. If you have a major, full-potential gap, consider a high-intensity initiative to bridge the gap, creating the platform for the next wave of adjacency expansion, rather than chipping away.

American Standard: How Core Focus Creates Adjacencies

Sometimes, even a single, hard-hitting, focused program to strengthen the core business can lead to adjacencies that would not have been otherwise possible and can fuel another wave of profitable growth. One example is the American Standard turnaround-to-adjacency-growth story, which is probably the best-demonstrated practice of a core focus that created profitable adjacency growth. As I spent a day with Mano Kampouris, the former CEO, learning the intricate details of American Standard's turnaround to growth, I marveled at the laser precision of his management team's method of improving their core and by the rich adjacencies that were liberated.

Over and over in these company profiles and CEO interviews, I was struck by the extent to which major changes in fortune could sometimes be traced back to relatively small beginnings or chance events. It is like the basic principle in biology, whereby "a tiny, almost undetectable mutation in the genetic blueprint might be enough to produce an enormous change in the organism as a whole. A few molecular shifts here and there might be enough to make the difference between brown eyes and blue, between a gymnast and a sumo wrestler, between good health and sickle cell anemia. . . . One tiny accident can change everything."[11] What was not chance in our business examples, as the American Standard story shows, was the management team's awareness of the opportunity when even the smallest glimmer of it did appear.

American Standard operates in three of the more basic businesses inhabiting a modern economy today—braking systems for vehicles, bathroom fixtures (especially bathtubs and toilet bowls), and air conditioners. The company traces its origins to the 1929 merger of the American Radiator Company and Standard Sanitary

Manufacturers Company. American Standard in 2002 attained $7.5 billion in revenues and $365 million in profits—a dramatic change from ten years earlier, when the company was on the edge of chaos, losing $116 million on revenues of $3.8 billion and facing a long-term debt load that was an astonishing 58 percent of revenues. Losses were increasing each year, and sales growth was less than 1 percent per year. Since the turnaround and subsequent IPO, American Standard has grown revenues at 9 percent, earnings at 14 percent, and the stock price from $4 (to ESOP holders) to $75 ten years later—a great return for such a basic business, or for any business.

Kampouris and his team were trying to figure out how to deal with the huge debt load placed on the company in its 1988 management buyout. They were sitting in a presentation being given by a consultant who had an approach to improve inventory flow. The management team recognized that the company had only two ready sources of cash. First, it could sell off parts of its business. Second, it could reduce inventory from high levels (sixty to ninety days for businesses with the then-typical inventory cycle of manufacturing plus shipping) to a much lower level never before attained in the industry. The consultant's system of demand-flow technology that was demonstrated in several plants in Japan, however, held out one hope. The key elements were the elimination of a series of handoffs so that more processes ran in parallel, the development of product teams versus functional teams, a search-and-destroy mission for non-value-added activities, and a new level of relentless repeatability (that phrase again) in operations. To accomplish this required a "big bang" program that would lead to turnaround or failure, since $500 million in cash was needed in two to three years from the working capital program to preserve the company. Kampouris comments on the result:

> So we took the plunge. Every one of our 110 factories was totally rearranged. We created a rigorous training program that 22,000 people went through in less than a year. We reorganized every manufacturing person into process teams. We put in place intense metrics regarding cycle time and quality

and changed our compensation system to focus on a single variable, inventory reduction, heavily linked to cycle time reduction. And it worked. We reduced inventory by more than 70 percent, turns increased to fourteen in the U.S. plumbing business, we saved over one-third of our entire floor space worldwide, our error rate in shipping and manufacturing declined, and we started to gain substantial market share because of our quality and speed of delivery (resulting in vastly improved fill rates)—a huge issue when you serve the construction trades. We created a ranking of every plant's cycle time and inventory reduction improvement and circulated that to every manager every month, and then we applied this same set of tools to the back office, where it worked, too. We had other companies visiting all the time, ranging from General Electric on to less-accomplished companies that wanted to see what we had done in this basic business to reduce our working capital so much.[12]

In the American Standard story, dramatic repairs of one key element of the core business generated major adjacency opportunities and fueled 8–9 percent growth in a market growing at a rate of 1–2 percent. For example, American Standard, with its improved manufacturing infrastructure, was able to go into the fixture and faucet business using its lower-cost plants in Mexico, Bulgaria, and the Far East—a share-of-wallet adjacency that was a natural add-on to sinks and bathtubs. This business grew quickly to more than $50 million in profitable revenues. In Trane air conditioning, the company had the cash to rebuild its service business and to start purchasing the sales and engineering units that it had franchised decades earlier. Since the turnaround, the service business was built from below $300 million to more than $1 billion of revenues. In its plumbing business, the improved cash position allowed the company to purchase Blue Circle in Europe. Finally, and especially important, American Standard had the capability to become a major supplier to the new, growing mass-merchandise channel epitomized by The Home Depot and Lowes. By virtue of the demand-flow improvements in accuracy and cycle time, American Standard became the leading supplier to The Home Depot in that category and won its Golden Hammer award as a top supplier—something never possible earlier. In the end, the American Standard story is impressive: four adjacencies liberated and made possible by the fixing of core economics.

Judging the Full Potential of the Core

How do you know whether you are at full potential in the core? How did Marcel Telles at AmBev know? Although there is no universal way of knowing for certain, there are some clear indicators:

- Poorly defined core, no consensus

- Declining core-customer share of wallet

- Flattening unit cost experience curves

- Increasing competitor reinvestment rates or market share

- Disappointing recent adjacency attempts

- Increasing product and process complexity

- Varying and unexplained performance differences across units

- Lack of revision of customer segments

These indicators emerge from examination of case studies in which greater potential was discovered in a core. If three or more of these apply to your business, it is likely that there is substantial additional potential. Probably six of these were applicable to Brahma when it was acquired in 1989.

For instance, Brahma had poor manufacturing productivity ratios relative to brewers outside South America. The company had been leaking market share to Antarctica and others and was shown to have declining customer satisfaction in surveys, a predictor of future leakage. It was earning much less than its cost of capital, a sign of underperformance for a leading-market-share brand. The fringes of Brahma's business were under attack from imported beers. And Brahma did not know its customer segments in the way that AmBev would later know them and use this information. Moreover, Brahma had been underinvesting in its infrastructure relative to what the best beer companies with leading brands were doing in other parts of the world. Finally, Brahma had not been managing its unit costs down over time. Combined with his direct observation of the culture and work methods relative to other companies, these indicators provided a clear picture of underperformance, given the company's competitive position and brand share in the market.

Carter's: Full Potential Through the Power of Fewer Things

The story of Carter's is an example that takes these ideas one step further and shows what can happen in a potentially strong core business when it layers new adjacencies on top of fundamental underperformance in the core. The example of Carter's also reinforces some themes of previous chapters regarding focus, repeatability, and the need to build adjacencies on a strong core. As such, it is a fitting concluding example for this chapter on assessing the state of the core business and working it to a point where it can take advantage of all the opportunities that adjacent moves can afford.

Usually, when I ask companies for their financial data, I receive the past ten years' worth of figures. Not so with Carter's, the leader in baby layette and sleepwear in North America. From Carter's, I received several sheets of paper with financial information going all the way back to 1889, still more than twenty years after its founding in 1865 by William Carter in Needham, Massachusetts. As you will see, the Carter's story provides a fitting conclusion to this section on practical management approaches to growth and adjacency expansion.

Having arrived as an immigrant from England's textile district, William Carter began the activities that in 1865 turned one cardigan-making knitting machine in the kitchen of his house into the William Carter Company. Among Carter's early products were uniforms for Union troops and underwear made of a cotton that was noted for its distinctive softness. This characteristic was received enthusiastically in a world where most undergarments itched mercilessly and was probably an inspiration for Carter's quote "If you sell good goods, they'll find you in the woods."[13]

If you look closely at the data sent by Carter's, you can almost feel the ebbs and flows of the U.S. economy. It is just like reading the seasonal patterns from the rings of a cross section of a single tree. In the 1929 crash, the steady, almost unbroken growth of thirty years suddenly gave way to a 62 percent drop in sales. The company did not recover from this drop until World War II, when its sales were partly bolstered by military clothing orders. In these data, you can then read the return of the GIs to the boom of families in suburban America and the consequent explosion of baby sleeper demand, which tripled the size of the company in only seven years, from 1950 to 1957. Prosperity brought rewards for new products and creative marketing. For instance, Carter's led the way in moving from the monotonous parade of pink and blue baby wear to a rainbow of colors—a move triggered, in part, by a personal appeal from Shirley Temple for garments in green, yellow, and purple for her own children. The demand for baby wear continued to grow steadily through the next twenty years, during which time the company quintupled in size.

Then in the 1980s, something happened. The company achieved a scale that outgrew its historic operating systems, creating high cost and inefficiency. More productive competitors manufacturing offshore were winning with cheaper goods. Carter's, in spite of its brand leadership, saw its sales slide from $219 million in 1984 all the way to $148 million in 1988, when the company hit bottom. This downslide induced the Carters to sell their family business to Wesray, the buyout firm, in late 1987.

The revival of Carter's to the growth success story that it is today is an appropriate way to end this section. The concrete actions the company took epitomize in a single case example one set of approaches, taken under huge pressure, to create conditions for relentless repeatability, to use complexity as a competitive weapon instead of a competitive liability, and to stabilize the core business. And the revival worked well: In a low-growth market (the growth of the baby population) the company reversed its slide, and then more than quadrupled its sales in the next twelve years, through organic growth alone.

When he took the helm of Carter's in 1988, CEO Fred Rowan found that the first order of business was fixing a core beset with problems. For instance, Carter's had 25,000 products in 1990, too many says Rowan:

> We had enough products for a $10 billion company; I physically could not get through the list. We had kimonos for children, fifteen different shades of navy blue, bodies with six pockets for babies who don't need pockets, and tons of zippers not needed on garments of that type. We had 500,000 dozen units of product that had been produced to keep the factories busy that had no orders attached to them sitting in the warehouse. We were the last fully integrated company of our kind in the United States, with plants that made yarn, plants that did cutting and sewing, and even an embroidery plant. Our systems were mostly manual. We were facing competitors producing offshore, with lean product lines, fast cycle times, and newer information systems. The business was near death operationally. The new management team had their moment of anxiety as we absorbed the magnitude of the challenge. Then, about five minutes later, we got down to work. Thankfully, we had one strong core asset to build around, and that was a key to it all: The company had never shipped bad quality and was still the number one brand in the consumer's mind.[14]

Over the next four years, it was "all hands on deck" to cut down the product line, take the necessary write-offs, close all domestic manufacturing facilities, move production to a low-cost location in

Asia and Central America without missing a season or a budget, and install new systems. After the turnaround, Investcorp purchased Carter's from Wesray, with the hoped-for value coming from growth, the core operational turnaround having been completed. Just having this improvement in the core alone drove revenues from $148 million in 1988, the bottom, to $318 million in 1996. This compound growth rate of 21 percent testifies to the power of improving the core around an undermanaged leadership franchise.

The next order of business was growth through close-in adjacencies in a highly focused way. The first target was the one hundred outlet stores with shrinking store sales, treated primarily as factory outlets. Though there were other possible targets, the management team chose this one. Rowan explains the choice: "I have done a lot of shooting with shotguns. My father used to say when five birds come up, pick one, knock it down, and then think about the second one. Getting overexcited about the number of targets is the most common mistake of shooting." Carter's changed store management, moving from factory outlet stores to professional retailing. It developed a store model that was operationally consistent and relentlessly repeatable, and got it to work through professional merchandising and a bold price reduction. The change worked, store growth turned around, and store profits grew even more, encouraging Carter's to build another fifty-five stores, fueling new growth.

It was then time to move into more distant adjacencies: new channels and playwear for older children. On the surface, moving into the mass-merchandise channel looks like a small change. But in reality, such a move is nearly a two-step adjacency, an area of danger, as we have shown, where many fail. Wisely, the management of Carter's, veterans of five stall-out-to-growth experiences, recognized what they were getting into and launched a major study of the economics of the mass-merchandising channel and of the differences of each of the participants, from Wal-Mart to Target. The company hired executives who had been successful selling to, and satisfying the needs of, each of these large customers, explains Rowan. "We discovered through this process that we truly did not realize the economic model in this channel—what it really took to win. There were profound details to do with pricing, restocking, information flow, distribution, and so on, that each had to go perfectly." To show the magnitude involved, Wal-Mart, at $230 billion in revenues, sells approximately $2 billion in clothing for young children. This figure represents five times the entire sales revenue of Carter's! And Target is not far behind in the category. Again, the requirement for adjacency success was massive attention to the required operational details and a relentless repeatability, product by product, order by order, into this channel.

Carter's faces many other interesting adjacencies, from international expansion (for which it so far has none) to other brands, other clothing, and other accessories for babies. Yet, it is determined to stay with the two adjacencies, the mass-merchandise channel and children's playwear (each with large potential and one to two steps away from the core), until it has mastered the detail of each and has demonstrated the repeatability necessary to grow in each category. Just that level of success alone could triple the size of the company.

As I left the building on my last visit to Carter's, I stopped to make a call in the conference room near the reception area. My eyes were drawn to a motto embossed on the wall near photos of children, the company's end consumers. It said, "Trust the power of fewer things." In some sense, the motto is one of the great lessons of growth strategy, well articulated in this company that has been growing for more than a century, experiencing extraordinary ups and downs, but always focusing in its own way on the franchise of clothing sleeping babies.

Adjacency or Core?

Certainly the matrix showing thirty-two different states of the core that opened this chapter could be embellished and made infinitely more complex. Yet, when we stand back from the mass of examples, interviews, and statistical analysis of success, a few universal principles of business emerge:

1. Major adjacency moves are virtually never the salvation for a very weak core in a distant follower competitive position.

2. For followers, the most viable paths to the creation of value entail consolidating with a competitor or finding deep within the business a strong, profitable core where the principles of full potential and adjacency expansion can be applied. In a sense, this is "shrinking to grow."

3. Adjacency moves are critical to the survival of businesses with a melting core.

4. Businesses that have a strong core but are severely underperforming operationally and financially should almost always work on attaining full potential of the core first.

5. Businesses that have a strong core or dominate a niche but are close to full potential are probably entering a phase in which the quality of their adjacency moves will shape their future.

6. Companies with a portfolio of core businesses should ask themselves whether they are defining the boundaries of those cores correctly, whether they really understand the competitive position of each business, and where each fits in the positional matrix of figure 4-1.

These principles underscore the importance of knowing the state of the core. This chapter has explained how companies can acquire and interpret this key information. Fred Rowan explains it well: "When I came to Carter's, I became convinced that we could only go into adjacencies if certain things happened in the core. Focus on the core is a disease. You have it or you don't."

Deciding on an adjacency move is one step in going beyond the core. The next chapter will discuss how to manage this decision once it has been made.

5

Executing Adjacency Moves

Managing the Key Organizational Issues
That Most Influence Success or Failure

Most organizations inhibit growth. Why? Organizations are often set up to protect the status quo, but growth is not about the status quo. Organizations tend to become more complex and more internally focused over time; each can stifle growth. The strongest core businesses have the muscle to retain their best people, as probably they often should. Yet the gravitational pull of the core can stem the flow of talent to new opportunities. At the same time, the opposite response of creating such a magnetic pull in the new, "hot" adjacency that it depletes or distracts the core can be equally harmful. These natural tendencies of organizations need to be managed if a company is to achieve sustained, profitable growth.

In a survey of 138 executives, 65 percent listed internal and organizational factors as the most influential reasons that new growth opportunities fell flat.[1] Nearly 60 percent of the executives felt that failing adjacencies were allowed to continue much longer than they should have been, sapping valuable energy. Almost half of the executives felt that inadequate management attention in the organization was a primary factor in adjacency failure. During several client projects focusing on how to accelerate the move into new adjacencies, I have been involved in interviewing managers to understand what they felt were the barriers to achieving their growth goals. In virtually every case, organizational issues emerged as the primary barrier, ahead of competitive moves, the viability of the plan, adequate resources, and new product performance.

The CEOs interviewed for this book returned over and over to organizational factors that they believed had shaped success or failures in their experience. Michael Dell says, "The unique structure of our organization makes it especially easy for us to move into new customer or product adjacencies. We have developed a formula for this that we apply over and over again, from reporting relationships to the transparency of our financial reports."[2] Tim Eller, CEO of Centex Homes, the major home builder with the best record of sustained, profitable growth, speaks of his company's organizational process: "Our new adjacencies always report to the CEO at the start in order to make sure that they get the proper care and feeding and to give us a chance to figure out the best long-term organizational solution. We spend enormous attention on the way that we later shift the business to become more tightly linked to the core, while trying to maintain enough autonomy."[3]

Andy Taylor, CEO of Enterprise, also stresses the importance of organization: "We have spent a lot of time working on how to organize ourselves in ways that keep the adjacency tightly linked and controlled by the core, but do not stifle independent thinking. We start new businesses in our strongest three markets first. I attend all business updates on our learning in the new business. We believe that adjacencies must have the best and the brightest, and we have learned that if we do that, we can keep accountability like we do in the core business. We want the accountability to be no different than in the rest of the business."[4] Victor Fung, CEO of Li & Fung, considered organizational structure paramount in any adjacency decision: "I have found that the organizational decision about whether to have an integrated business or to keep a new adjacency separate from the core is among the most important factors in determining success and one of the toughest judgments to make, sometimes as important as parts of the strategy itself."[5] Virtually all the CEOs went out of their way to stress the organizational challenges of adjacency expansion.

CEOs with the most successful adjacency track records felt that their company's insights on organizational issues actually created proprietary sources of competitive advantage. These insights clustered around the answers to a few key questions: Should the adjacency be set up separate from the core or be integrated? How can I balance the need for independence and protection of the adjacency with the need for linkages to the core? Does it ever makes sense to permit a distinct culture to persist in the new adjacency, or does that balkanize my company? How can I make the way we move into adjacencies more repeatable and efficient through the processes that I set up to manage them? What is the best way to identify and exit from unproductive adjacencies without being perceived as giving up too soon? What does this adjacency require to be successful in its own right, given the gravitational pull of the core?

Unlike the previous chapters, which were laden with empirical data, this chapter is based primarily on the case examples and direct comments of senior executives who have grappled with these organizational concerns, which fell into three clusters:

- Managing linkages between the core and adjacencies

- Organizing for repeatability to exploit the new math of growth

- Exiting adjacencies

Managing Linkages to the Core

Organizations, if left to their central tendencies, do inhibit growth. They have immune systems that create their own version of antibodies that attack something new entering the body. Yet, the best growth companies have discovered how to control these inhibitors. Consider, for instance, this list of seven adjacency moves by companies interviewed and cited in this chapter. On the surface, as you scan the list, you will find that it is not easy to decide how an adjacency move should be organized relative to the core business. The right answer can only be discovered through immersion in the details of the linkages to the core.

- STMicroelectronics's entering the flash memory business

- UPS's entering the service parts logistics business

- Centex Homes's entering services like mortgages to homeowners

- Dell's entering the printer market

- Staples's entering the delivery business for small enterprises

- Enterprise Rent-A-Car's entering the truck rental business

- Lloyds Bank's entering the personal insurance business

All the preceding adjacencies were successful. Yet, the organizational approaches spanned the full range, from Dell's and Enterprise's full integration in the core, to Centex's initial separation and direct CEO reporting relationship, to hybrid organizational models for Lloyds, Staples, and UPS. Often, the relationship between the core and the adjacency evolves over time with experience and maturity. The online retail business of Staples began as a totally separate entity next door to its headquarters, even with a separate public stock, and was eventually absorbed back into the core.

The Lens of Shared Economics

Three analytical lenses have proved to be particularly important in looking at an adjacency and trying to understand how it links to the core. It is easy to look superficially at two businesses—say, the sports beverage and juice businesses (the situation in the disastrous integration of Quaker Oats, owner of Gatorade, in its purchase of Snapple beverages in 1994)—and believe that on the surface these businesses must have a great deal in common. Surely, you might say, the products are both nonalcoholic, noncarbonated beverages sold in retail stores, delivered in bottles, and consumed by thirsty people. Yet, a more detailed exercise of combing through the cost structure, step by step, would reveal that the production processes are totally different between Snapple and Gatorade. The customers are actually quite different, as are the required advertising, the locations of purchase, and therefore the distribution networks.

Understanding the extent to which the new growth initiative and the core have overlapping, or shared, customers and the extent to which they have common types of infrastructure, or shared cost, is important in making the right organizational choice. This sharing can be quantified and is often quite revealing. For example, the ability of GE Capital to purchase and integrate about two hundred acquisitions successfully over ten years emerged from its ability to recognize patterns of shared economics and develop a repeatable formula for swift and effective integration.

As a rule of thumb, an adjacency move with less than 25 percent cost sharing but high customer sharing would usually be set up quite separately, though with highly choreographed sales and marketing activities, and maybe even a combined sales force. One example would be how Centex Homes entered the mortgage origination business in the 1980s. Initially, this new adjacency reported to the CEO and served, almost entirely, Centex's own core customers, who were purchasing homes built by the company. Over time, the business expanded in scope. As Larry Hirsch, the current chairman of the board of Centex, said, "The emergence of a national mortgage market and the securitization of mortgages really helped us to grow the business with confidence. This is an adjacency that mushroomed, was then further separated into pieces such as a pure retail mortgage business. Today we are 80 percent retail, and only 20 percent [of mortgages are for] our own homes. Profitability is higher for our own homes, the original reason for the business. But in all segments, the business needs little capital and the returns are impressive."[6] This lens of cost and customer sharing is a good starting point for understanding more deeply the linkage of an adjacency and the core. Then, organizational design can ensure that those areas of overlap are managed correctly at the inception as well as in maturity.

The Lens of Shared Decisions

At Bain & Company, we use a tool called RAID as the starting point for tackling certain organizational issues. RAID takes the most important decisions that an organization faces—decisions about pricing, new products, major spending, and customer positioning—and diagrams exactly the choreography of how those choices are made and who makes them. The acronym stands for the ways that a decision can be influenced: recommend, agree, input, and decide. This tool can quickly reveal when key decisions have no clear "owner" or when decision processes are too complex or vague or when there is insufficient structure for decisions to be made with all relevant sources of input. A simplified version of this approach can provide important guidance on how a new adjacency should tie in to the core business. Typically, twenty to fifty major decisions might initially be identified and examined.

Some of the most intertwined decisions between the core and a new adjacency are moves into new channels or new geographical areas. Both types of adjacencies can sometimes touch the same customers, making marketplace coordination especially critical. Tom Stemberg, founder and former CEO of Staples, one of only ten companies to reach $3 billion in profits in less than ten years, comments on one experience:

> Taking a proven, well-defined core into another geography seems like a relatively easy adjacency on the surface. Yet, when you actually go out and try it, even in places as similar to our original geography as Canada, the litany of failures

that have gone to Canada and fallen flat becomes apparent. For example, every package in Quebec has to have French on certain parts of it, so none of our packages for office products worked there. About 90 percent was the same, but 10 percent was totally different, and if you get that 10 percent of detail wrong, you automatically fail. Having a corporate core that is nimble enough, a local management that is balanced enough, and an awareness of these decisions that is detailed enough to pull this off correctly is really hard.

Today Canada is our highest-market-share country and one of our most successful expansions economically, reaching highly profitable revenues of over $1 billion. Yet, it took longer, was more costly, and was much, much harder than we ever imagined. If that is true of Canada, for a format as well proven as Staples, imagine how hard it is when you go even a step farther away with a less proven concept.[7]

Over time, Staples has become more and more aware of the detailed decisions that drive the success and failure, the speed and delay, of an adjacency move. This awareness of the myriad of details that ultimately determine success and the ability to plan for it separates the best growth companies from those that stumble while shifting from concept to execution. Identifying and mapping out the key decisions can be a surprisingly valuable first step toward the development of a repeatable method, so often emphasized in this book as the root of much value creation from adjacency expansion beyond the core.

Identifying the most important joint decisions between the core and the new growth business is a critical first step. The second step is to work out who gets to make the decision—the core or the adjacency. Consider the situation of a company's branching out into another country, such as when Staples moved into Canada and Germany; RE/MAX, the leading residential realtor, took its real estate model into Turkey, where it now has branches; or Enterprise Rent-A-Car moved into the United Kingdom. For Staples, office products differ substantially in Germany and even in Canada from those in the United States. How much standardization should be imposed, and how much local discretion should be allowed? For RE/MAX, real estate commission structures differ dramatically in Turkey compared with those of the United States. As a result, RE/MAX changed its economic equation substantially, but was steadfast in maintaining the way the company provides training, tools, and services in the branches to the agents. Enterprise Rent-A-Car found that it could maintain its operational practices (delivering the car; small, low-cost locations; suburban focus), hiring practices, and internal measurement and bonus practices and drive those centrally. On the other hand, policies related to fuel charges and interactions with insurance companies were dramatically different. Indeed, the company had to virtually work for years to try to shape the practices of insurance companies by which policyholders were assisted with obtaining alternative transportation when their car was in the body shop for repairs. In each case, there is no uniformly correct answer. But there is a correct process that starts by identifying the linkages, determining which are most important, and then tailoring the decision ownership and inputs accordingly.

The Lens of Shared Culture and People Systems

Cultural issues and other factors related to people management were highlighted in nearly all of the interviews and case studies as a top concern of CEOs moving into new adjacencies. Cultural factors alone were cited by 51 percent of the executives in our broader-based survey as a primary factor in adjacency disappointments in their experience. And cultural issues are cited in public accounts of a significant percentage of acquisitions and expansion programs that encountered problems. Examples include the disastrous acquisition of The Learning Company (East Coast software) by Mattel (West Coast toys) and the continuing saga of how the AOL Time Warner merger achieved virtually none of the synergies that were targeted at the time of the merger.

Here are some examples from our CEO interviews:

Enterprise Rent-A-Car: CEO Andy Taylor began our discussion describing the business and cultural origins of the company his father started. He said his adjacency criteria are now biased away from acquisitions. "Our culture is so strong that it is easier to start new growth initiatives ourselves at this point. Our culture will simply overwhelm in the end, is a huge competitive differentiator, and [sits] at the top of our list of growth considerations. When I look at the most critical elements to transfer into new adjacencies, it is the way we select, reward, and manage people, and the values from our strong culture."[8]

STMicroelectronics: CEO Pasquale Pistorio spoke at great length about how this amazing European semiconductor company has built its culture around a clear set of five cultural values, which he ticks off in rapid fire: "Our culture is central to all we do and is built around five principles that everybody, everywhere goes through: (1) the obligations of leadership, (2) the meaning of empowerment, (3) the importance of the most fact-based decision making in all we do, (4) recognition of continuous improvement in all we do, and (5) the most vital point of customer focus. The customer is the only one who sends the product to the field, the only one who gives us revenues that make us prosper, and the source of most growth opportunities. Everything we train for, everything in our culture, ultimately revolves around the customer."[9] ST has built its growth around a relatively small number of deep alliance partnerships like the one with Nokia. Pistorio describes at length a customer-centric culture that is central to most adjacency expansions his company has undertaken and to the way it thinks about finding new sources of growth.

AmBev: CEO Marcel Telles talked in detail about how he had to build a new type of performance culture before attacking new growth adjacencies. He also discussed the wide array of creative practices used to reinforce that culture and transfer its value to new adjacency expansions in other brands, other beverages, or other geographies. "What we really did first was focus on the culture and the systems related to the motivation and management of people. I had learned this in my investment banking experiences where all the assets virtually went down the elevator every night. We really focused on this and still do."[10]

UPS: In answer to my question "What is most distinctive about the strengths of UPS, bearing on the approach to adjacency growth?" CEO Mike Eskew also pointed to cultural factors: "We are very strong in our culture. This is the first thing that comes to my mind. While the trucks are all brown and the delivery requirements are fixed, how our employees get the job done in their parameters is up to them. There is huge integrity and trust among our employees and between the customers and us. It is a strong heritage of Jim Casey. He gave us the guidelines that we translate to new businesses like Service Parts Logistics. The unifying concept is a culture that is built around making our customer better."[11]

Each of the companies just mentioned possesses strong, almost monolithic cultures that shape the way in which the respective management teams think about adjacencies in and around their core business. In each case, the strong culture is infused into each adjacency, becoming a way to reduce complexity and ambiguity. Sometimes the way the cultural norms are best infused into an adjacency is not by having the adjacency "owned" by the core, but by having the adjacency run by someone with intimate knowledge of the core culture. That person will value and embed the key values of the core without compromising areas in which independence is critical. For example, the UPS service parts logistics business was run by Bob Stoffel, a young engineer who had grown up in the core "brown truck" delivery business and was well respected by the executives running it.

It is not always appropriate to extend the core culture or even the core systems around people management, but it is always appropriate to invest time in making this determination in the most careful way possible. Sometimes the right answer is a temporary, if not permanent, separation of the adjacency and the development of a unique set of cultural norms and people management practices. Jim Vincent, chairman and former CEO of Biogen, highlighted one such example from his experience in growing the Abbott Laboratories diagnostic business from $10 million in the 1970s to a highly profitable, leading, $3 billion business today:

> One major adjacency experience in my career was the development of the Abbott Diagnostics business. They had been playing around with a small division of one hundred people and $10 million in sales after twenty-five years that was dedicated to using radioisotopes for diagnostic medicine. The business began [in Oak Ridge, Tennessee, in 1948] with a single scientist who had a passion for this method. . . . When I arrived, it was starting to encounter new competition as others were seeing this as an area for investment and the business started going downhill. I was asked to lead an effort in my first year to figure out what to do with the business.
>
> So I jumped on it. We turned it around quickly in its current context and then started to look at future directions. We studied closely the experiences of other pharmaceutical companies that had tried to get into diagnostics as an adjacency to their drug businesses, and . . . we could see why those efforts were unsuccessful. They had tried to impose a large pharmaceutical company culture with its detailing force and long R&D lead times on what was a hardware business, not sold to the doctor, with a much shorter cycle time, and higher technology. Yet, large pharma was the antithesis of the culture of a high-technology company. We recommended building the business globally, turning it into a higher-technology business built around hardware and reagents, and especially recommended that it be totally insulated from the mother culture because we would be doing things that would seem crazy to everyone else.[12]

As a result, the business was kept separate, a distinct culture developed, and Abbott Diagnostics became the leader over several decades. Yet, it drew carefully upon linkages with the Abbott Laboratories core. It used the brand name of Abbott, which was critical to its credibility. It shared the physical distribution network and international network to move the product around and store it, and it shared some key technology. Vincent describes one such process: "An example is the critical hepatitis B test. A lot of the fundamental research on hepatitis was from one individual who had done work on the key antigens over decades. We felt that technology could make it into a diagnostic test, too. And it was. My bottom line from this experience? Study your organizational and cultural issues very carefully as to whether the differences required in the new adjacency are too great. In my experience, this is the primary reason why most adjacency moves fail. To get this done right, it had to report directly to the CEO to give the business an independent status that let us create this different culture." The result created tens of billions of dollars of value.

The development of Intel, and the company's constant struggle with the question of how to separate new adjacencies while still linking them enough with the dominant core, has been well documented by Robert Burgelman. He points out that the core business is referred to as the creosote bush within Intel because, like the desert plant that secretes a sap that kills or engulfs everything near it, Intel's powerful microprocessor core can have the same effect on new adjacencies. One executive, referring to the power of this core, said, "Intel is the world's largest single cell organism." Burgelman points out that "the creosote effect made it difficult for the new business to thrive. The reason for this was simple. Any technology advance that enriched the PC environment was likely to create more demand for microprocessors. Thus, it was generally more valuable for Intel to give away technology and quickly disseminate it in the market, rather than try to build a business around it."[13] CEO Craig Barrett's response to this dilemma was to create two new units reporting directly to him, the Network Computing Group and the New Business Group. This arrangement allowed him to manage the core and adjacency linkages more directly. The Network Computing Group has been highly successful because of this separation. The New Business Group proliferated investments during the Internet bubble of 1999 to 2001 and is continuing to sort through its investments, understanding better their true potential and linkages to the core. Intel is an extreme example of how one of the strongest and most dominant core businesses on earth can complicate the task of planting and fertilizing the right seeds for the next wave of growth.

A group of my colleagues at Bain recently conducted a study of the extent to which cultural issues can be managed in adjacencies made by acquisition. Looking at 124 deals from 1996 to 2000, they concluded that there was a 14 percent difference in stock price performance between companies that identified cultural integration as critical during the due-diligence phase and addressed the issue in integration and the companies that did not. They argued that these problems are even more severe in service businesses, whose primary assets are people, and in cross-border transactions with multicountry operations, both of which are growing trends in mergers and acquisitions.

Options for Combination with, or Separation from, the Core

These three lenses—shared economics, overlapping decisions, and cultural fit—can assist in developing the options about how to organize the new adjacency. The range of options to link an adjacency with the core organizationally is vast; those that were favored most often by the companies in this book are listed below.

1. *Complete separation:* Integration of decisions occurs primarily at the level of the CEO. Consulting firms, including my own, have entered the private equity-investment business as an adjacency that was totally separated and reporting to the managing partner. This is how Bain Capital, now a

large, totally separate, and highly successful company, was structured when it was first launched by founder Bill Bain.

2. *Back end integration with front end separation:* Three of the six types of adjacency moves—new customer segments, new channels, and new geographies—are, at their core, marketing- and sales-driven initiatives that often draw upon a common set of back room operations and infrastructure to produce the product. In these cases, the adjacency would draw almost entirely upon the infrastructure of the core business. When Enterprise Rent-A-Car moved onto the airports to serve its customers there, expanding from suburban locations, it used the same back end IT and fleet management infrastructure for each. When Staples set up its delivery operations to serve business customers, it used the same back end purchasing, IT, and warehousing for each. When Vodafone moved into retail stores to serve its customers directly, it fed this new channel with the same service and technology platform it used to distribute through other channels.

Conceptually, these choices sound obvious, and the implied structures sound relatively straightforward. However, to really push the boundaries out successfully into these new adjacencies there are still an enormous number of linkages between the core and the adjacency that need to be considered and worked out. The Dell example cited earlier of the foray into the indirect channel (on top of its direct distribution) in 1993 and 1994 is an excellent example of an adjacent move with a shared back end (manufacturing, product development, IT, marketing, advertising), but separate front ends (sales force, freight). What was discovered in the process was the incompatibility of serving both channels well at the same time. This revelation was embodied in the difficulty of making and implementing effective and compatible decisions on a range of specific and detailed operational matters like pricing, customer sales interactions, and manufacturing scheduling.

Thorough consideration of how these decisions will work in detail is critical no matter what organizational structure is established to knit together the core and the new adjacency.

3. *Back end separation with front end integration:* Businesses whose core is centered on serving a focused set of customers and whose growth comes from increasing share of wallet in that customer, or following that customer's needs through their life cycle, represent the classic case of back end separation and front end integration.

   PETsMART's initiatives to use the store's network to sell services to pet owners in addition to products is a classic case. The new service business is managed separately from the product infrastructure that feeds the stores with a stream of hard goods and pet foods. Yet, the services of grooming, training, and boarding pets are implemented at the store level by the store manager. The detailed choreography between the back end and the front end must work perfectly to ensure that the service business is accepted by and integrated into store operations, while still maintaining a separate identity to develop, track, and test new products.

   Another example from the interviews where this type of structure is called for is STMicroelectronics. Manufacturing companies that serve a highly focused group of large OEM customers like Nokia need to have a highly coordinated and integrated account team consisting of salespeople and technical experts. This integrated team, in the case of STMicroelectronics, has found that the number of back end sources of products has increased over time as the company has added new capabilities in order to serve its core customers' expanding needs in developing "systems on chips." For example, ST entered the flash memory business to serve its existing customers, adding back end research, development, and manufacturing capacity, but selling through its existing frontline account managers.

Once again, the basic structure in this situation sounds obvious, but it is the details—how multiple product and technical organizations on the back end interact with an integrated front end customer-facing organization—that determine ultimate effectiveness of the business and success of new adjacencies bolted onto the core business in this way.

4. *Complex hybrid:* Some companies employ a highly customized structure in which the adjacency has its own sales force, but also has mechanisms to make combined sales calls on major accounts and shares some infrastructure with the core, but not all. The UPS service parts logistics business, discussed later in this chapter, is an example of a complex hybrid that works well.

5. *Product management model:* This is a simpler structure in which most services, customer-facing activities, and infrastructure are completely shared with the core. The core business manages the adjacency directly. An example is the truck rental business of Enterprise Rent-A-Car. The truck business had its own fleet, sales specialists, and financial reporting, but all its other functions were integrated in the car rental regional structure. Certainly, many adjacencies of P&G, like the Crest Whitestrips and the SpinBrush described in an earlier chapter, would fit this model.

6. *Complete integration:* Here, a new adjacency moves as rapidly as possible into full integration with the core on every dimension. This is probably the final stage of evolution for companies like Vodafone, which is assembling a global network and standardizing the customer service experience and branding.

No mechanical formula exists to define the right way to link an adjacency to the core. However, the questions regarding shared economics, shared decisions, shared culture, and shared people systems that shape the best solution are relatively clear. Sometimes the right solution might be to have the adjacency start in an independent

FIGURE 5 - 1

Core Versus Adjacency: Determining the Degree of Integration

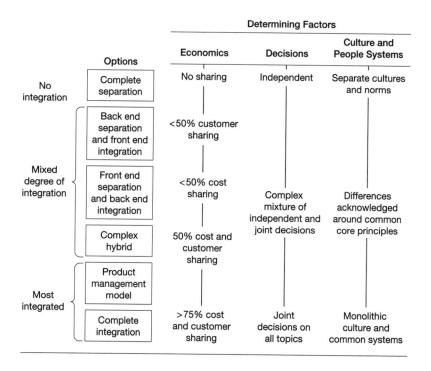

	Options	Determining Factors		
		Economics	Decisions	Culture and People Systems
No integration	Complete separation	No sharing	Independent	Separate cultures and norms
Mixed degree of integration	Back end separation and front end integration	<50% customer sharing		
	Front end separation and back end integration	<50% cost sharing	Complex mixture of independent and joint decisions	Differences acknowledged around common core principles
	Complex hybrid	50% cost and customer sharing		
Most integrated	Product management model			
	Complete integration	>75% cost and customer sharing	Joint decisions on all topics	Monolithic culture and common systems

structure, reporting directly to the CEO, with the plan to gradually shift into the core; or the plan might be to have the adjacency incubated in the core and, when stronger, spun off with a new independence. What is crucial in determining the long-term solution is the degree of sharing along the different dimensions just described. Figure 5-1 summarizes the range of options and the range of sharing between the adjacency and the core that should be considered in determining the best of these options.

UPS Service Parts Logistics: Success from Managing the Linkages

The movement by UPS into the service parts logistics business is an example of a hybrid solution to the organizational issues just described, as well as a dramatic demonstration of how fast a major adjacency can be developed when the issues regarding shared economics, decisions, and culture are determined quickly and effectively.

United Parcel Service is the leading private shipper of small packages in the world, with $32 billion in revenue. Since its IPO in 1999, UPS has grown revenues at an annual rate of 6 percent and earnings at an annual 15 percent. Such high growth rates have been an increasingly tough challenge in a core market that is growing at below 5 percent per year. In order to maintain its growth momentum, UPS has been pushing out the boundaries of its core business, step by step, into new areas, from the tracking of software to the financing of trade to logistics management and consulting. Since 1996, revenues from these new adjacencies have grown from near zero to more than $3 billion. The jewel in the crown is the entry into the rapid distribution of critical parts, the service parts logistics business, now a part of what UPS refers to as its Supply Chain Solutions group.

The story of how this opportunity was identified, evaluated, and implemented shows clearly how critical it is to think through the linkages to the core business, to assess full potential with hard facts, and to move quickly once the concept is proven. In discussing the actions taken to enter service parts logistics, Mike Eskew sits back for a while and says, "You know, what I especially liked about the business was that when all was said and done, it felt like an extension of what our founder, Jim Casey, would have done. We used our network in a new way to bring scale and scope to customers around the world. [The new business's] origins were in the requests we were receiving from customers to enter this business so they would not have so many different shippers and systems for each element of their own business. However, there were a lot of tough choices and decisions along the way, many relating to how this new adjacency would link to the core. Getting the details of that right, or setting in place early a process that would look at new details and make the best judgment for UPS, was critical."[14]

To understand what service parts logistics (SPL) entails, consider the following question: What do you do if you run a brokerage business and your hard drive crashes, or run a hospital needing patient results from a sophisticated diagnostic machine that suddenly breaks down, or head an engineering firm whose design workstations freeze because of a network failure, or run an airline with costly planes constantly needing spare parts? The costs of these delays are potentially enormous. For instance, downtime for a Wall Street brokerage firm could run more than $6 million per hour in lost or delayed revenue. So the answer is that your equipment suppliers must figure out how, at almost any cost, they can get the right parts in the hands of a competent repair technician as fast as possible. But how do they know exactly the right part? And how do they stock critical but scarce and costly items? This high-customer-value problem is what the UPS service parts logistics business is designed to handle, whether through shipping services only, or through full parts and logistics management and outsourcing.

Since 1995, the business has grown from a $61 million business called SonicAir and acquired by UPS to a nearly $1 billion business with strong momentum and linkages to the core everywhere. How did it get from there to here?

Eskew and his team launched a project to understand the full potential of the service parts logistics business—just how good could it be? Service parts logistics originally was budgeted to grow to $230 million in revenues in five years, a healthy rate of growth, but could it be more? The answer from extensive fieldwork on the market revealed that the business had more than ten times the expected potential. The customers desperately wanted better service from vendors they could trust with one of their most vital functions. The market was diffuse, with no particularly strong competitors worldwide. Service levels were not high, and systems were inadequate to track information or predict time delays for customers. This performance level provided a major opportunity for UPS to invest in its improvement, thereby creating real value and competitive differentiation. The poorly documented market (excluding inventory cost and repair expenses) totaled a whopping $18 billion and was growing at 9 percent worldwide, about twice the rate of the core. UPS reacted to the new data by immediately assigning a team of sixty people, led by one of its best logistics engineers, Bob Stoffel. The team's charge was to develop and implement an aggressive plan to obtain the full potential for UPS and on a time schedule that would catch competitors by surprise and preempt an investment response.

The physical part of the strategy involved building infrastructure at a rapid pace. UPS purchased seven parts logistics companies in the next three years, completed joint ventures in India and Japan, and completed the development of a global call center network with four primary locations and six specialized satellites with multilingual capabilities. And it began integrating the results of highly successful selling efforts at customers into more than six hundred field-stocking locations for parts on six continents. The result was growth (half organic, half acquisition) from only $75 million in 1997, to nearly $1 billion in 2002. By its preemptive investment, UPS captured a leading market position six times as large as the next competitor in the United States and better than parity worldwide. You just don't find adjacency expansions off a core business that do much better than that.

In the engine room of this strategy, however, was immense complexity and a long list of absolutely critical questions that the new business had to address with regard to its linkage to the core. Getting this right was as important to the strategy as anything else. How would the new service be sold—through the UPS sales force, a separate force, or a hybrid of the two? How would the UPS brand be used—as a sub-brand, not at all, or as local brands? How would the UPS package infrastructure be applied, since the acquisitions used UPS for only a modest fraction of their shipments? Would SPL standardize on UPS tracking and information software? Where would SPL report in the organization—to the CEO separately or to the core? These are just a few of the dozens of critical questions that needed to be identified and addressed.

The original premise was to keep the businesses relatively separate, but as the team studied this further, one linkage to the core at a time, a more complex solution emerged. At one extreme, service parts logistics was required to utilize the UPS delivery infrastructure, brand, and sophisticated tracking software. In between were customer strategies, sometimes a service parts logistics sales force, sometimes joint calls with SPL as a specialist, sometimes a joint account plan as a customer. Internal processes needed to be set up to monitor and constantly adjust the customer strategy. In fact, the team discovered that SPL often created excellent leads for the core business and that this became a competitive weapon for the core, especially in Europe, where the UPS presence in the core business was less than in the U.S. market. At the other extreme, SPL had to develop its own engineering prowess tailored to the specific and unique needs of parts logistics. These unique engineering aspects included multiple direction flows (parts come back from the field as well as go to the field), predictive algorithms of parts to send to the field, and management of a highly distributed stocking network very different from the core UPS package distribution system. The culture and values were intensely integrated, and the business reported to the CEO directly at the start.

During the rollout, the team set up processes to monitor and manage these linkages. Meanwhile, new issues such as customer offerings, pricing, cost sharing, and information management emerged from experience. Management of these complex linkages was probably the deciding factor in the level of success of this adjacency expansion.

Organizational Repeatability and the New Math of Sustainable Growth

Understanding and acting on linkages is critical in increasing the odds that an adjacency move will be successful. A further multiplier factor is the ability to take the lesson of repeatability in growth moves, discussed in chapter 2, and translate that into how often the organization attacks new growth opportunities, captures the learning, and refines the process for the next one.

As a constant reminder of the unknown, you can use the simple framework of drawing a box with four cells in it. Each cell represents your perception of information on a topic in terms of conscious and unconscious understanding. So, one cell is "what you know you know," a second is "what you know you don't know." For this exercise, the most important cell is "what you don't know you don't know" (the pure unknown). People vary greatly in terms of how they divide up the box into these four areas, with the most mature and experienced decision makers typically found to be those who believe the pure unknown is enormous, and need to factor in time and open-mindedness to deal with that uncertainty. In situations of decision-making uncertainty, I sometimes reflect on this framework, asking myself, "Am I really so sure?" The world is inevitably more complex, I conclude.

Thomas Kuhn, who devoted his career to exploring scientific methodology, which culminated in his book *The Structure of Scientific Revolutions,* cites a game of a related but slightly different nature. Subjects were shown playing cards in rapid sequence and then asked to recall them. Some of the cards, however, were distorted, such as a red four of clubs or a black queen of hearts. As the game slowed in pace, the subjects began somehow to realize that they did not know all they thought they did and became quickly disoriented. The simple retreat to what they knew from past experience was no longer working. Then, finally, they recognized that there were, in fact, new details and patterns that needed to be understood.[15]

Adjacency expansion from a core business is, by definition, a move into the unknown. In many case studies and interviews with companies that experienced strong growth through adjacency expansion, I asked about success rates and about a notable single instance of failure. On average, these companies had experienced success rates of more than 60 percent, far beyond the 25–30 percent average. When discussing an adjacency that had fallen short, the executives believed that for more than 75 percent of the cases, the adjacency was inadequately understood in advance. They also believed that further information could have been obtained for these cases and might have changed the level of preparedness, if not the decision itself. At the center of all these discussions was the topic of complexity—the adjacencies were inevitably laden with details of the category "things we did not even know we did not know."

Tim Eller of Centex Homes describes how much more could have been known about the business model for prefabricated home sales before Centex entered and then withdrew. Biogen's Jim Vincent describes the foray by Texas Instruments, years ago, into lower-end consumer electronics. The move was a financial disaster because of a wide range of details inadequately examined. Pius Baschera of Hilti describes the company's aggressive entry into lower-end construction and fastening products. The company did not fully realize the differences in business economics in this new segment, from which it later withdrew. Nick Shreiber reflects on Tetra Pak's entry into the plastic blow molding business: "We entered way behind as a distant follower. More homework on the requirements for good economics would have driven us towards buying one of the leaders, or taking a totally different approach."[16]

The Role of Complexity Management

We also used the paired comparisons to examine the importance of complexity. We looked at the number of types of moves, the number of moves, the number of moves to new platforms, and the average distance from the core of each move—all divided by company size—to make some assessments of complexity. We then combined these numbers to obtain a very rough measure of complexity. Using these crude indexes, we found that the slower value creators had complexity levels that were 91 percent higher than the faster value creators. The laggards made moves that were less repeatable and seemed to shoot off in more directions.

As the many companies' stories have shown, the management of complexity can be distilled into these three steps:

- Focus on important complexity

- Shed extraneous complexity

- Develop repeatable routines to handle necessary complexity

A further confirmation of the central role of complexity management came in the growth survey of the 138 executives cited periodically throughout this book. The survey asked these executives about the root causes of disappointing adjacency moves. Seventy-five percent said that unanticipated implementation challenges were a major cause of failure, more than any other single category of response, which ranged from inadequate resources to unpredicted external factors or competitive moves. Sixty-eight percent agreed with the statement that "adjacency moves have proven to be much more complicated than we anticipated."[17]

Finally, there is the record of major public disappointments among the most complex adjacency strategies. One prominent example is the AOL Time Warner merger that targeted $1 billion of synergies from a range of specific areas, from subscriber growth to new products using Time Warner content to advertising. Virtually none of the targeted synergies have emerged, and the market has seen this, causing the stock price to underperform the Standard & Poor's media index by 55 percent from January 2000 through the end of 2002. Complexity, false hope, and the inability to anticipate the details that blocked these synergies are an all-too-common story in many "grand strategies" (i.e., strategies for which projections bore no resemblance to actual occurrences).

The implication is that methods to reduce the management complexity, much of it unanticipated, when a company is moving into new areas of growth can be extremely important in increasing the odds of success as well as the speed of execution. If half of your growth comes from moving into new adjacencies around the core, and you can cut in half the time of decision and implementation, then, on average, your growth rate should increase by one-third. If repeatability makes you more reliable, there is a further multiplier effect.

The New Math of Sustainable Growth

Companies that outgrow their core competitors for extended periods often do so because they have more success at moving into new adjacencies around the core. This success may be due to a fundamentally stronger core. It may also be due to better selection and implementation on those adjacencies that permit (1) higher success rates, (2) faster ramp-up to success, (3) greater ability to achieve the full potential of an adjacency move, and (4) the ability to handle more (perhaps because of repeatability) moves of a given type. All these performance levers can be improved by better managing both "good" and "bad" complexity.

To see this more clearly, we returned to a simple computer model that looked at a company that was growing organically at 3 percent, a typical market growth rate for a large proportion of companies. We then calculated the longer-term impacts on revenue and profit growth from different rates of adjacency expansion of the core. The base case is quite modest: investment in two adjacencies per year, a 35 percent success rate, a three-year ramp-up, and achievement of only 50 percent of the potential value per adjacency, which we set at 10 percent of the business size. (Think of a new channel, entry into a new country, purchase of a business that makes complementary products, and so on.) Under this relatively modest assumption, the 3 percent growth business would double its growth rate of revenue to 6 percent and its profit to 7 percent. From here, moving from two to three adjacency investments and increasing the success rate to 50 percent triple the base growth rate to 9 percent and the profit growth rate to 12 percent. The assumptions we used were not inconsistent with the type of investment or success patterns observed across the different sets of companies we examined. The upshot of these numbers is simply this: Moderate improvements in the success rate or the speed of execution translate into substantial changes in growth.

The point becomes even more powerful when coupled with the extent to which the stock market values improvements in reliable and balanced growth. On average in the 1990s, a publicly traded U.S. company growing at less than 5 percent in revenues and profits would return to shareholders an average of 4.1 percent per year. If that growth is erratic and unbalanced—profits without sales or sales without profits—even a fourfold increase in growth (un-balanced) only doubles shareholder returns. Yet, balanced growth is where the premium is. A company that moves from the 0–5 percent growth category in revenues and profits to the 5–10 percent category will triple its shareholder returns from 4.1 percent to 12.4 percent. Over ten years, this is an increase in shareholder wealth of 320 percent versus only 148 percent for the lower growth rate—sort of a double multiplier effect for successful but consistent adjacency expansion strategies versus the big move or the inconsistent pattern of growth.

Speed of execution, reliability of execution, and reduction of the cost of failure are each critical to the way that adjacency expansions create value. These are the reasons why a relentlessly repeatable ad-jacency formula can have such powerful economics, competitive implications, and the ability to transform a core business.

The theme of complexity appeared over and over in the case studies and the CEO interviews regarding successful and unsuc-cessful adjacency campaigns. It appeared in planning, where adja-cency moves were always found to be more complex than antici-pated. It appeared in idea sourcing, in which deeper drill-downs into understanding of customers yielded more powerful new growth opportunities than the broad concept. And complexity appeared in execution, in which understanding and managing the organiza-tional linkages between the core and the new adjacency in detail loomed as so critical.

The Hidden Costs of Underperforming Adjacencies

Andy Taylor reflected for a while before he came up with an answer to my question regarding his most important role as CEO of Enter-prise Rent-A-Car in adjacency expansion initiatives that sought new growth from their core replacement rental car business. "Often my most important role is to say no, to cry out 'Stop! Let's think.'"[18] Every adjacency, in process or in proposal, has its advocate and its argument. It is human nature to feel optimism in the presence of the excitement of a manager sponsoring or trying to keep alive the flame of a new growth initiative. Bill Monahan, CEO of Imation and a former senior executive at 3M, a company built of technical adjacencies, speaks of this enthusiasm: "The definition of an adjacency suggests that someone in your organization is in love with it. When you kill a project, you run the risk of telling an evangelist in your organization, 'Thanks a lot for all your effort, but we don't think this is good for the company any longer.' That is hard to manage and easy to avoid doing. . . . Under the old 3M culture, not enough was killed and this eventually created enormous complexity and cost."[19]

More than half of the companies interviewed indicated they believed there was a natural human tendency to let adjacencies go for far too long. Nick Shreiber of Tetra Pak describes how his company adopted a more critical attitude toward innovation: "Tetra Pak has tightened up its structured approach to innovation with more rigorous return maps and milestones for projects we are funding. We have found that the toughest thing of all is to shut down projects. We do much experimentation, and we hate closing down a development project. In the past five years, we have shut down more than in the prior twenty years, as a result of this. One consequence we are now seeing is greater remotivation among the R&D group because people are immediately reassigned towards projects with a higher degree of success. So, there is still shock and resistance to shutting things down, but more recognition that it has to be done."[20]

The unproductive adjacencies have hidden costs. One cost is the obvious financial and human cost of resources that could be invested elsewhere in the core or a more promising adjacency. One hundred percent of the executives interviewed said that the supply of growth ideas was not a problem; the biggest problem was deciding on the right ones, turning them into viable economic propositions, monitoring their progress, and implementing them. Forcing the core to cross-subsidize problem adjacencies is a dangerous trap. Some of the great turnaround-to-growth stories examined here, such as STMicroelectronics and Carter's, began with the new CEO's triggering an initiative to reduce product lines, eliminate complexity, and withdraw from misconceived adjacencies.

A second, and more subtle, cost of a problem adjacency relates to a company's commitment to results. As Tim Eller of Centex says, "Letting a problem adjacency linger for too long begins to suggest to others elsewhere in the company that it is suddenly all right to lose money."[21] Michael Dell referred to the danger of conceptually seductive but uneconomic adjacencies as "the trap of profitless prosperity." Setting an economic standard takes years and can quickly be compromised by inattentive or hesitant management of unprofitable adjacencies.

Finally, there is the cost of complexity from managing a portfolio of too many adjacencies, especially when some are problems. Few companies maintain data that look at the portfolio of growth investments as a whole, array those that are close to or far from the core and look at returns, or even do a periodic appraisal of historical data to understand their own success rates. Few companies even know their own success rates.

Muzak: Getting Its Groove Back

The case of Muzak is a stark illustration of a company that entered the wrong adjacency, let it persist for too long, and triggered an extended period of stall-out and strategic malaise in the core business. A new owner acted quickly to exit and then trigger several new adjacencies with virtually immediate effects on growth, focus, energy levels, and health of the core. The message is echoed by Andy Grove, founder of Intel, in discussing adjacency moves: "Though you are always uncertain in business, you must act on your temporary conviction as if it is a real conviction. But when you find you are wrong, correct it right away."[22]

Muzak was founded in 1934 to commercialize a system patented by inventor, George Squier, and designed for transmitting phonograph music over electrical lines. The first major use of the new technology was in elevators to calm riders, who were unaccustomed to this new invention for vertical travel that required them to enter windowless boxes that rattled and made unsettling noises. Muzak was, truly, elevator music, even though none of the company's sales today are for that purpose. The applications have shifted to the piping of music into malls, retail stores, restaurants, doctors' offices, and anywhere that music can create a mood, dampen sound, or help to reinforce a brand identity.

Since its founding, the basic economic model of the business has not changed that much. A music format is selected by the customer and piped into the business, usually through equipment that Muzak provides. The average contract creates an annuity with a six-year life. Though it looks like a simple business to replicate, the barriers to entry are actually quite high, including (1) the national sales force for service, very important to customers and not easy to set up for such a niche business, (2) one of the best-known brands, such that the word "Muzak" is part of the language now, (3) a low-cost infrastructure with high customer switching costs, and (4) the ability to deal with music copyrights—a complex and arcane science requiring enormous attention to detail. For instance, the fine to a company for a single violation in one location of a copyright is $10,000. That could add up to big costs for a retail chain in repeated violation.

Muzak grew slowly into the early 1990s, when it was acquired by a private equity firm that proceeded to try to engineer a breakout from the core music business into a major new adjacency. The one the firm chose was the use of the network of transmitters and signal distribution to sell other information products like educational courses to retail employees or the delivery of daily updates of needed business information. Unfortunately, this adjacency built not on the true competitive differentiations that are the mainspring of the business, but on the common carrier distribution system that many others could replicate. Getting digital information to a business location can be done in many ways. The secret was in the management of customized music.

One officer at Muzak says today of this initiative: "This took all of the senior management time and most of the investment resources for a full five-year period, from 1993 to 1998, trying to crack the business-to-business communications market [and] trading on a common carrier platform. This was not the differentiator in the core business, however, and it was not at all where the leverage for profitable growth was to be found."[23]

As a result of this initiative, growth slumped to zero for the next five years. In 1998, Muzak was purchased by ABRY, a highly successful private equity firm specializing entirely in media. A new strategy was quickly developed and put in place with three major components. The first was the immediate exit from the failing adjacency. Every employee in that unit was released at the close of the sale to ABRY.

The second element of the strategy was a refocus on driving the full sales potential from the core music business, a profitable business that had experienced disinvestments for the previous five years. Management analyzed the potential customer base in a new and much richer way. It looked at the way customers used music in their business (to reinforce brand, as background only, for unique customization, for a certain type of music, etc.) and the propensity to purchase high-quality music. This led to recognition that the market was larger than had been believed, and that a narrower focus on fewer segments, but with a sales force doubled in size from ninety to 180, could fuel growth for a long time to come. The sales force was retrained in Muzak University (whose motto is "Selling is more important than spelling") and taught to use new laptop computers loaded with new selling presentations that included a clever simulation device that could match music formats to a video of the customer site. These actions in the core selling engine increased new revenue per salesperson (new contracts) by 100 percent and drove growth in the core quickly from zero to 15 percent.

Third, the management and new owners found two adjacencies that actually built on the true differentiator of music. Both adjacencies showed the value of deep customer research in uncovering market segments that are underpenetrated or unappreciated. One was an opportunity in the new-customer segment of home-office workers or small-office workers who want to use music to professionalize their phone interactions, including the possible insertion of customized messages along with the music. The product is called "music on hold" and has become Muzak's fastest-growing product line. Initially, this product was sold and installed by the company, a costly proposition for a relatively low-priced product. However, Muzak has developed packages so that customers can easily install their own with just telephonic assistance, making this product now quite attractive economically. The other example comes from more precise segmentation of the customer base, identifying a set of users for whom music is integral to reinforcing an image or a brand. For instance, a retailer like Gap might have customized music related to its fall sweater collection (issue: what music is most associated with sweater weather?). The ability to customize, deal with copyrights, distribute real-time to store systems, change music with events or clothing collections, and occasionally weave in messages is a product that many sophisticated chains want.

During the adjacency misadventure from 1993 to 1998, Muzak's revenue and profit growth were zero. From 1998 to 2002, in remarkable contrast, the company increased 52 percent in revenues and 84 percent in operating earnings and had a stream of new opportunities teed up for further growth—all stemming from the decision to exit the failed adjacency. This example of how Muzak "got its groove back" shows in detail the creative and destructive potential of adjacency expansion, as well as the potential for rigorous customer segmentation to uncover new opportunities that build on the true strengths. Above all, the example highlights the cost of entering the wrong adjacency and, especially, letting it persist and sap energy from the core. The swift reaction of the new owners shows how much energy exiting the wrong adjacency can liberate.

Confronting the Paradox of Organization

Three themes emerged over and over in CEO discussions and in more detailed analyses of organizations trying to execute on an adjacency expansion. One theme was the value of mapping out the detailed linkages between the adjacency and the core and using this information to decide on organizational structure, reporting relationships, and the decision processes.

The power of repeatability and the high economic value that accrues to an organization that can execute faster and more reliably on adjacencies was a second consistent theme. This allows the value to be captured faster, enables companies to handle more adjacencies over any period, and increases the odds of success. Our simple model shows how even modest improvements in all these dimensions, each driven by repeatability, can magnify each other as they compound over time into extremely large differences in final value. It is like the lessons of fast cycle time in manufacturing applied to strategy execution of growth initiatives. One way to grow faster is to carry out each growth initiative faster and more reliably and then to get on to the next one sooner. This is no surprise, but the magnitude of actually doing it can be surprising.

The final theme concerns the need to exit disappointing adjacencies soon enough. Exiting adjacencies reduces management complexity and frees up resources for more productive activities. The active management of exits can also reinforce a culture of performance in an organization.

Attention to detail, the implantation of clear performance standards for growth, the insistence on rigorous analysis of economics, and high metabolism of organizational reaction time are common attributes of companies that handle these critical issues of execution well. Most people think they act quickly and are rigorous, just as every professional golfer probably thinks he or she strives for repeatability and practices a great deal. But it is when you confront the standards of the masters, like Ben Hogan's relentless repeatability, that these entreaties become truly meaningful. There is little value in asking yourself in isolation, "Do I pay attention to detail?" More valuable questions are "Do I pay attention to detail as assiduously as the best at mapping out the organizational linkages?" "Am I as aware of the power of repeatability and the math of growth as the masters?" "Am I as decisive as the best in pulling the plug on resource-absorbing failures?" It is these issues that are on the minds of the best CEOs, who invariably choose to err in the direction of more decisiveness and more rigor. As Jack Welch has said many times when asked what he most regretted over the course of his career, "[I regret] that I did not act fast enough, often enough."[24] And this is the CEO of a company noted for its process rigor, its bias to action, and its decisiveness. So, it is not enough just to believe you are fast-acting, rigorous, and detail-oriented. You must compare yourself to world-class companies on these dimensions of organizing for growth.

6

Transforming Through
Adjacency Moves

Redefining the Core Through Adjacencies

Most companies do not live for very long. The average life span of a company in the major industrial economies today is only about twelve years, down from more than twenty-five years for companies in existence in the 1950s. A study by *The Economist* suggests that the ultimate life span of even established multinational corporations is only about forty years, with life ending in takeover or bankruptcy.[1] For companies in the *Fortune* 500 today, this would imply that one-third would no longer exist as independent entities just twelve years from now—all once-strong companies that somehow failed to adapt their core fast enough to even more rapidly changing market conditions.

Of course, survival alone does not create value. Only two of the twenty-seven companies in the Forbes 100 seventy years ago that have survived have outperformed the stock market. One view of this sobering data is that companies are meant to be ephemeral; they are set up to serve a short-term need in a dynamic world. Maybe, the argument would go, companies should not live for very long. In fact, they should live incredibly hard and fast lives. The cost, but not necessarily the timing, of their demise should be minimized. Alternatively, a more balanced and contemporary view is that organizations are extremely costly to create and to dismantle. Therefore, the best outcome would be if the best organizations could learn to adapt to their conditions faster, become obsolete less often, and create value for a longer time. One way they could do this is by redefining their cores. But how?

The primary reason that companies die or tumble into extended periods of value destruction is not because their market suddenly disappears. Nor is it because their market persists, but becomes uniformly unprofitable. Rather, it is because those companies were overtaken by competitors. They had failed to adapt, and failed to redefine the core. Even some of the longest-lasting markets, from oil production to home building to automobiles to clothing, contain a range of companies—some highly profitable and some highly unprofitable. One analysis that we conducted found that only about 20 percent of the variation in profitability levels among companies related to the specific choice of market that they participated in, leaving 80 percent for company-specific factors such as performance relative to their competitors.

Of the twenty-five larger companies examined most closely for this book, twenty had experienced periods of stall-out or even near death. The same number had origins that went back more than twenty-five years. The companies studied in this book were selected because of their performance, not because of these other criteria. The companies with long histories and then sudden inflection points, or even turnarounds (some of them to ten-year profit performance in the top 13 percent of companies worldwide and far above their industry average growth) spanned a wide range of industries. They included American Express, Tetra Pak, Li & Fung, Lloyds Bank, UPS, Enterprise Rent-A-Car, and Tesco.

Throughout our analysis, most companies that made dramatic transitions to periods of sustained, profitable growth had an underlying strong core business that was turbocharged and subsequently found a method to push out beyond the core consistently and profitably. Vodafone redefined its core by choosing first a geographic vector, moving into leadership, or near-leadership positions in twenty-two localities over twelve years. IBM redefined its core by moving along the value chain again and again into new service segments, starting with the most basic integration and repair services for its own hardware and eventually reaching up into value-added consulting services. Dell also redefined its core. It evolved from a company selling personal computers to technophiles on the phone in the United States to a $40 billion company selling and integrating complete corporate systems to global enterprise accounts. AmBev redefined itself from coleadership in the Brazilian beer market to clear leadership throughout the South American beer market. The next waves of adjacencies in other beverages (Guarana Antarctica, for example) and a wider range of brands, on top of its dominant distribution system, offers the promise of the next phase of transformation to a continent-wide drinks company.

Each of these companies redefined its core over time through a long sequence of related moves in a common direction, or united by a common strategic theme. Both the massive, singular move and the leap to a totally new business are spectacular when they succeed, but they rarely do. The most significant redefinitions in our study occurred when all four key factors for the most successful adjacency expansions (articulated in chapters 2 through 5) coexisted. This concluding chapter looks at the multiplier effect when all the following factors are in play at the same time (figure 6-1):

1. A strong core on which to bolt adjacency moves

2. Adjacency moves that satisfy the three key criteria (relatedness to a strong core, robust profit pools, and the potential for leadership economics)

3. A repeatable adjacency formula or franchise

4. Adaptable and replicable organizational processes to manage adjacencies

FIGURE 6-1

**Transformation Through Adjacencies:
The Four Multiplier Factors**

1. Strong or dominant core	2. Adjacencies that satisfy criteria	3. Repeatable adjacency formula	4. Replicable, adaptable processes to manage adjacencies
	• Potential leadership economics • Robust profit pool • Relatedness to the core		• Complexity management • The new math of execution • Exit management

A dominant core or, at a minimum, a strong position in a channel, a customer segment, or a product line in a weaker core is the first requirement for successful adjacency expansion. The availability of moves that satisfy the three key criteria established in chapter 2 is the second condition. When your options fail to link tightly to the core, fail to target a robust profit pool, or never have the potential for leadership economics, you have the ingredients for future value destruction. Though these criteria look obvious, as discussed earlier, many companies struggle with establishing criteria (as the comments by Sir Brian Pitman before the Lloyds turnaround showed), and even more companies find it difficult to assess growth initiatives factually and objectively. The best companies seemed to be the most rigorous in deciding when to fund a growth initiative. Given a core to build on and a menu of potential moves, the third level of the game occurs when successful moves begin to suggest a series of similar future moves, as in the case of Nike (a complex hybrid collection of moves). The final level of the game occurs when the organization can literally mobilize internally to have repeatable processes in which the organization need only make small changes to successfully implement movement into a new adjacency. This book closes with two examples of companies in one of the most basic and enduring of all industries—the construction and sale of homes and other buildings. I choose this industry because it epitomizes the classic profile of a large, traditional, fragmented, modest-growth market.

Centex Corporation is a central Texas home builder whose performance was good, but not spectacular, for over thirty-five years. Its moons then aligned under new leadership, and a new growth strategy emerged, resulting in a surge of profitable growth and, in the process, a redefinition of the core. The changes occurred through strategy, leadership, and execution, not external market forces.

RE/MAX, a privately held real estate agency company, took nearly a decade to establish its business model, gain market acceptance, and stabilize the core. Then the company took off, growing its core organically at the same time that it expanded into geographic and service adjacencies to move from start-up to the leading company in its industry. Again, you can see the door to expansion blow open as the four key factors click into place, like the tumblers of a combination lock, unshackling growth potential.

Centex Homes

Probably one of the oldest of all businesses is the construction of homes. Yet, even here, there exist examples of business transformation when these four elements have come together. Centex Homes is today the largest integrated home-building, homeowner services, and construction company in the United States. It is in the top thirty of the *Fortune* list of America's Most Admired Companies for 2002. Yet, like so many of the companies profiled for this book, Centex had modest beginnings and a long period of modest financial performance, followed by a totally different period of profitable growth and transformation. Here are some of the numbers:

	Revenues	Earnings
1982	$1.1 billion	$28 million
1992	$2.2 billion	$35 million
2002	$7.7 billion	$382 million

In the decade from 1982 to 1992, Centex expanded its revenues by 100 percent, but earnings grew by only 20 percent. In contrast, the following decade, which culminated in Centex's fiftieth year as a company, revenues increased 280 percent and earnings skyrocketed 990 percent. The market value of the company had increased by a factor of 4.6, nearly twice the performance of the S&P 500 index over this time. Not bad for a company in one of the most basic and most low-growth major industries.

Centex began in 1947 through a chance meeting in a Dallas bank lobby between founder Tom Lively and oilman Ira Rupley. Lively approached the older man because he was holding a rolled-up set of building plans, and Lively wondered if he and Rupley had something in common. The two decided to combine forces to create the Rupley-Lively Construction Company to build starter homes of two bedrooms and one bath, priced at about $10,000 to $12,000. By mobilizing quickly, they could take advantage of the sixteen million veterans returning after World War II with access to advantaged VA and FHA loans that allowed them to purchase a home with no down payment. The company was incorporated in 1950 as Centex, standing for Central Texas, the focus of their strategy.

During the first thirty-five years, the company's financial performance was relatively undistinguished. Its primary accomplishments were the development of a growth platform consisting of its strong home-building core in the Southwest of the United States, the creation of a few beachheads in other locations like Puerto Rico and Florida, and the establishment of a general construction subsidiary (primarily apartments, industrial parks, and shopping centers). Along the way, Centex invested a great deal of time and money in a wide range of unrelated adjacent businesses, from cement to concrete pipe to aggregates to natural gas to chemicals.

Almost all these diversifications have been divested, allowing the company to focus in a more single-minded way on the construction core and to drive into adjacencies that reinforced the core, rather than sapping resources and attention from it. After Larry Hirsch became CEO at Centex Corporation and Tim Eller subsequently became CEO of Centex Homes, the company's strategy shifted. It focused on closer-in adjacencies to home building and the construction business and put in a rigorous control system that emphasized return on capital, even for the growth investments. On this same topic, Larry Hirsch, currently chairman of Centex, discusses some of the disciplined approaches the company takes:

> Our experience with adjacencies and our success in the core business is making us become more discriminating and tightly focused with respect to investing in adjacencies, even though we are many times larger than just a few years ago and have high growth aspirations. In fact, we are now going through business by business to make sure that we are still the best parent. We have had greater success with growth at the same time as we have become more conservative about accounting, about expensing everything, about capitalizing nothing. We require that our investments hit a return-on-capital hurdle that we monitor constantly, and even apply this to the new adjacencies. Otherwise, we are not interested, given all that we can do in and around the core. We set our hurdles depending on maturity, which we define as Phase One, Two, or Three, and we do not tolerate new initiatives that do not get to reasonable profitability within three years.[2]

Soon, the key factors for core redefinition were all having an impact on Centex. First was the strong core with more leadership economics on which to build growth. In 1985 Centex had 60 percent of its construction revenues in the Southwest, where it was the clear leader in home building and general construction, and had built strong niche positions in other locations as platforms for new growth. Today the percentage in the company's original core region has declined to 31 percent by moving successfully into surrounding regions. Also over this time, return on equity has increased by a factor of four.

Second was the application of much more rigorous economic criteria in the evaluation and tracking of growth investments. The team developed a new intolerance for growth investments that could not achieve profitability within a two-year time frame, and an increased willingness to exit adjacencies that were not on a path to attain the company's economic hurdle rate.

Third, the company really began to hit on all cylinders as it developed a more repeatable method for moving into new segments of the construction market and rolling out that capability to its strongest regions. Centex ended the 1990s with strong or leading positions in health care construction, educational construction, and mall construction, for example. Again, Hirsch comments on this:

> Our best success with serial, repeated adjacencies was actually in the core contracting business. Over time this has shifted much more towards specific market segments and functionalities, especially in the past five years. So, you do not just want to be a general contractor; you want to be an education contractor or a health care contractor or a mall contractor in order to develop expertise—real competitive advantage—and to focus the organization. We began with a regional general contractor focus with a few strong regions. Then, we would get into new specialty areas through acquisition and grow by first focusing on the strongest regions. Only when successful there would we branch out into adjacent territory. We have followed four specific principles in moving into new areas: First, build around the greatest geographic strengths. Second, focus and build around a few relationship customers in those geographies first. Third, later add in very focused value-added services in these specialty areas. And fourth, pay for performance. Regional leadership creates more margin. Industry scale with subcontractors creates margin and the ability to spread fixed costs. The economics of density creates margin in each of these specialized areas of contracting. This is the ultimate formula for adjacency expansion in our business and is highly repeatable in each of the movements into new areas of contracting. These are tough businesses, highly competitive, not tolerant

of failure, where systems are critical, scale is critical, and culture is critical. However, since the markets are so large, if you create real competitive advantage, you can grow profitably for a long time, as we have shown.[3]

Finally, Centex has developed a consistent and repeatable organizational method of handling new regions, new specialty areas, and new movements into a region in a particular specialty. Over time, said Hirsch, Centex has learned which linkages to the core are the most critical to the economics and which are secondary, and the company has tailored its processes and organization to these priorities: "The lack of synergies among the adjacencies and with the core has surprised us as we have grown. There are less synergies between the different businesses that do not have common customer types. The most powerful synergies are across regions with common customer types or across products within a region that have common customer types, such as mortgage lending, the title business, home building, and insurance, which are all builder based."[4]

The transformation of Centex from a regional home builder in the Texas area to a leading national construction company illustrates in a single story many of the book's points about the formula for sustained, profitable growth through adjacency expansion. The Centex story also illustrates how even a long-standing company with average performance in a low-growth and competitive industry can assemble the right elements and apply the formula, with dramatic results.

RE/MAX

From building homes, we move to selling homes, the primary job of the real estate agent, and to a company that has transformed not only itself dramatically through its growth strategy, but also its industry. RE/MAX is today the leading real estate brokerage company in the United States and probably the world, a lofty perch in another extremely competitive industry. And it is another example of a company in which, for a while, all four preconditions for the fastest value creation through adjacency expansion and subsequent transformation seemed to align. Since its start in 1973, RE/MAX has grown from one agent to 82,000; from one city to international positions; and from one service (selling homes) to a range of services, from buyer brokerage to mortgages to title insurance.

The company began as a maverick that was breaking the traditional formula for commission structure, in the face of massive industry protests, lawsuits, and disruptive competitive tricks. In the face of this upheaval, RE/MAX wound up setting the new formula that the rest of the industry has been forced to adopt, a formula that favors the ultimate producers, the agents. In his opening comment on the RE/MAX story, founder and chairman of the board Dave Liniger reveals satisfaction with the company's success: "The RE/MAX story is a phenomenal success story, but my competitors' stories are even more spectacular tales of failure."[5] Liniger hit the right industry at the right time with the right new model, no doubt. But his execution, sense of focus, and relentless repeatability epitomize another way in which our four multipliers of growth can be explosive when they coincide.

> What RE/MAX did is change the economic model in a way that especially favored the strongest producers and made them want to join. When we started, the agents were on a fifty-fifty split with their brokerage company, usually a regional company owned by the founder. The company would pay the expenses [and] insurance and provide an office. The company would keep [its] half and make a profit. The best regional companies were incredibly profitable under this model and made a fortune off of the best producers. RE/MAX said we would run like a cooperative and split the expenses of the office, providing training and advertising in return for a management fee to the company.
>
> The end result was that the agents were now keeping 85 percent of their commission. It was like being in business for themselves, but not by themselves. Naturally, the best agents

wanted to join the most. That is why, though we have 18 percent share of agents in Canada, we have 38 percent of the residential market and why, though we have 7 percent of the National Association of Realtors (NAR) membership in the U.S., we have 16 percent market share. Our agents average twenty-four transactions per year. Our main national competitors average twelve per year, and the rest of the industry is below seven transactions per year per agent.

Gaining significant market share in the real estate business happens when agents leave one company and move to another, taking their clients and relationships with them. Local businesses in which people changes are required for market share changes are often the toughest of business street fights. But few would seem better suited to persist in that environment than Liniger. He describes his beginning:

> I started as a teenager who dreamed of being rich, though I was a farm boy and the son of middle-class parents. I read *Think and Grow Rich,* about a postman who had become a multimillionaire by buying housing units. I went to college, but did not have the discipline. [I] left, and went to Vietnam as an airman. I returned, married, and worked three part-time jobs. Then one day I bought a single-family house for a $435 initial investment, fixed it, sold it, and made $4,000 profit. The die was cast. I started with a local brokerage firm in Denver, but left because I thought I had a better way to do it, and started RE/MAX.

Liniger's propensity for risk persists to today, making him a tough competitor. He learned to race NASCAR (National Association for Stock Car Racing) at the age of forty and soon rose to the top ten on the circuit, part-time. He trained with the Soviet cosmonauts to try to be the first to circumnavigate the globe in a hot-air balloon, falling barely short at the end. And he pushed out the boundaries of RE/MAX into one new adjacency after another, getting better and better at repeating and refining the formula.

Beyond the Core

Adjacency expansion is a specific method to achieve growth. It is different from market growth, from diversification, from venture capital, from cost and price cuts, from combining with your main competitor, and from programs to improve the loyalty of current customers. Yet, adjacency expansion is what CEOs today identify as the primary way they hope to achieve their next major wave of new growth. As we have seen, the potential is great to create value from well-executed moves that push out the boundaries of a strong core business. This book cites dozens of examples of immense value creation through thousands of individual adjacency moves along the way. By contrast, 75 percent of the greatest business disasters from 1997 to 2002 were either triggered, or worsened, by major adjacency moves that went horribly wrong.

The range of possible moves is great, the conditions under which they can be made vary widely, and the number of starting positions of the core are numerous. No silver-bullet formula exists. But there are clear risk factors and clear success factors in decision, in organization, in the search for repeatable patterns, and in execution. If this book simply clarifies the questions that need to be addressed and that are addressed rigorously in many of the most successful growth companies, then much of its objective will be achieved.

Some truths are eternal, such as the power of focus. The inherent tension between focus and growth will forever lie at the heart of some of the most difficult judgments in business or, for that matter, all organizations. Andrew Carnegie was one of the world's most successful businessmen of the last two centuries. During a talk to the students at the Curry Commercial College in Pittsburgh in 1885, Carnegie was asked to impart his formula for business success. His answer reflected the timeless and universal tension that is central to the ideas in this book. Even in light of the many contemporary examples and statistics just presented, his formula has a ring of truth today:

Here is the prime condition of success, the great secret: concentrate your energy, thought and capital exclusively upon the business in which you are engaged. Having begun in one line, resolve to fight it out on that line, to lead in it; adopt every improvement, have the best machinery, and know the most about it. The concerns that fail are those that have scattered their capital, which means that they have scattered their brains also. They have investments in this, or that, or the other, here, there and everywhere. "Don't put all your eggs in one basket" is all wrong. I tell you "put all your eggs in one basket, and then watch that basket. . . ." It is easy to watch and carry the one basket. It is trying to carry too many baskets that breaks most eggs.[6]

When the Scottish-born magnate sold his business, Carnegie Steel, to J. P. Morgan in 1901, Carnegie was deemed the richest person in the world. His company became the core of U.S. Steel, a company that persisted for a century, built on a dominant core, but expanded into product and geographic adjacencies with a repeatability that epitomized the word *relentless*.

The phrase *beyond the core*, the title of this book, is meant to signify this tension between the comfort and sensibility of focus and the allure and marketplace necessity of moving forward into the unknown. It is the companies that balance these opposing forces the best to whom the value creation of the future will belong.

Afterword

In writing this book, I have tried hard to balance the need for brevity (since the target audience is busy executives) with the inherent complexity of the topic (since the question of how to find new growth is potentially monumental in scope). As such, I have crammed into a dense package a lot of different findings that emerged from mountains of research, along with dozens of examples to illustrate those findings in the words of the executives who were there at the time. Yet, in spite of that distillation, if I had to titrate down several more levels to the key messages that could be delivered during the proverbial "elevator" conversation, it would be these.

1. Profitable growth is hard to achieve and getting harder to find. Pressures from investors to set high targets and the swift stock market penalties for shortfalls have never been greater. The temptations are great to set high targets that are unrealistic, with the danger of forcing large, imprudent moves beyond the core in an attempt to meet goals. It is no accident that 75 percent of the major business disasters of the past decade were caused or worsened by failed adjacency expansion moves.

2. Pushing out the boundaries of their strong core businesses is the primary way most CEOs expect to find their next wave of profitable growth today. Yet three-quarters of such

growth initiatives fail to drive profitable growth. Companies even within the same industry vary dramatically in the proportion of growth initiatives that succeed. The different records in the odds of success and the cost of failure go a long way to explaining differential performance. While there is no guaranteed "silver bullet," it is clear than many of the most important factors can be well understood and influenced by management and their processes.

3. A strong core business (or segment to build upon) is the most important driver of successful adjacency expansions. A weak core business is the most powerful predictor of failure. Strength in the core is measurable and tangible and almost always traces back to low unit cost or low systems cost to the customer. Growth and low cost are not opposing forces, rather they are complementary, even essential, for the long-term coexistence of each.

4. Most companies believe they have rigorous criteria for evaluating growth opportunities, but do not. Study after study shows how easy it is for management teams to fail to agree about criteria and objectives, often never knowing that this is the case. Some of the best CEOs at driving adjacency growth have been most insistent on starting here. The turnaround to growth story of Lloyds TSB under Sir Brian Pitman is a case in point.

5. The three most important economic criteria to evaluate are the robustness of the future profit pool, the degree of relatedness to a strong core, and the potential to achieve leadership-equivalent economics (especially in the area of cost). Yet these are the areas where the least fact-based assessments are often made, sometimes at great peril.

6. Relentless repeatability was at the heart of many of the most successful growth strategies and was a key explainer of the outcomes from some of the most dramatic competitive bat-

tles. Having a successful, repeatable formula allows companies to leverage the "new math of profitable growth" rather than having to hunt and peck at the periphery of their business for the next move. The divergent paths of Nike versus Reebok in the 1990s show the power of repeatability.

7. Many of the best adjacency decisions are the decisions to say no.

8. Major adjacency moves are almost never the solution for a weak core business in a stable market and almost always a critical option for companies with strong competitive positions whose market is deteriorating.

9. Most of the lasting and profitable adjacency strategies come from deep rather than broad insights. Deep insights most often emerge from detailed analysis of existing core customers using one or more of five key "lenses."

10. Organizations naturally resist change and create invisible antibodies to new growth. These organizational and cultural factors are not mysterious, but are predictable. They can be identified by studying the details of how the core and the adjacency need to be linked in the organization's decisions and their cost structures.

11. The most powerful way to transform a core business is through repeatable adjacency moves off a strong core that are executed by an organization built to constantly adapt and replicate the formula.

In summary, these major growth choices are among the most potentially profound in shaping the future of companies. They are also the most difficult decisions to make, because of the emotions involved, the complexity surrounding these choices, and the uncertainty about the future.

So often, initiatives to push out the boundaries in the search for new and profitable sources of growth lead back to the origin and to a greater understanding and obsession with leveraging and remaining grounded in the core while, at the same time, moving out into the unknown.

This book shows that many of the greatest disasters in the search for new growth were triggered by prematurely abandoning the core while a company leaped into the unknown or, on the other hand, by timidly remaining secluded in the core when environmental conditions were demanding boldness for survival. I hope that the ideas in this book and the CEOs' descriptions of their own lessons with adjacency expansion can help other management teams achieve a balance, avoid disasters, and attain new waves of profitable growth.

Appendix

Companies Researched for the Book

During the course of the research, our team profiled more than one hundred companies and spoke with the executives at those companies. Some were studied for highly focused reasons, others, such as the two lists below, were screened more comprehensively as part of the core analytics in the book.

Twenty-five Targeted Companies

These twenty-five companies were chosen because of their performance and their strategic approaches to adjacencies. They were also selected because they represent a cross-section of industries and geographies. I applied the following criteria to my selection:

- The companies had outgrown their core markets

- The companies earned the cost of capital in a period of adjacency expansion

- Revenues exceeded $500 million

- The companies had experience with adjacency growth

- Senior executives were accessible for interviews

North America	South America
American Express	AmBev
American Standard	
Best Buy	**Europe**
Biogen	Hilti
Carter's	Lloyds Bank
Centex	STMicroelectronics
Dell	Tesco
Enterprise Rent-A-Car	Tetra Pak
Nike	Vodafone
Procter & Gamble	Voith
PETsMART	
RE/MAX	**Asia**
Staples	Legend
UPS	Li & Fung
	Olam

Paired Comparisons

These company pairs were selected for analysis of the role of adjacency strategies in performance because of various factors:

- Industry similarity

- Publicly available data

- Different performance trajectories over a ten-year period

- Degree of focus (not conglomerates)

- Clearly different adjacency choices

Industry	Fast Value Creator	Slow Value Creator
Airlines	Continental	Swissair
Athletic shoes	Nike	Reebok
Computers	Dell	Compaq
Construction	Centex	Ryland
Defense technology	British Aerospace	Marconi
Drug distribution	Cardinal Health	McKesson
Energy/utilities	Duke Energy	Florida Power & Light
Engineering	Jacobs Engineering	Fluor
Grocery	Tesco	Sainsbury
Insurance	Aegon	Aetna
Insurance	AIG	Zurich
Retail	Walgreens	Eckerd Drug

Notes

Preface

1. Bain & Company and the Economist Intelligence Unit, "Global Survey of Executive Perceptions and Intentions About Growth," October 2002.

Chapter 1: The Growth Crisis

1. Andy Pasztor and Jeff Cole, "Low Orbit: Loral Chief Schwartz Seeks One More Feat: Salvaging Globalstar," *Wall Street Journal,* 26 January 2001, A1.

2. Jack Welch, panel discussion and discussion with author, Bain Getting Back on Offense Conference, New York, 20 June 2002.

3. Jim Vincent, interview by author, Boston, 4 June 2002.

4. Tom Stemberg, interview by author, Boston, 12 April 2002.

5. Pasquale Pistorio, interview by author, Milan, 18 September 2002.

6. Victor Fung, interview by author, Seoul, 17 October 2002.

7. Richard Miles, "Lloyds TSB," *Times* (London), 10 November 1997.

8. Brian Pitman, interview by author, London, 23 January 2002.

9. A. G. Lafley, interview by author, Boston, 26 November 2002.

Chapter 2: Visualizing the Ideal

1. Sunny Verhese, interview by author, Singapore, 22 October 2002.

2. Lafley interview.

3. Pistorio interview.

4. Vincent interview.

5. Fung interview.

6. Andy Taylor, interview by author, Teterboro, NJ, 27 June 2002.

7. Pistorio interview.

8. Pius Baschera, telephone interview with author, 19 July 2002.

9. Taylor interview.

10. David A. Garvin and Artemis March, "Harvey Golub: Recharging American Express," Case 9-396-212 (Boston: Harvard Business School, 1996), 2.

11. Phil Francis, speech to the PETsMART Leadership Forum, 2002.

12. David Lenhardt, interview by author, Boston, 11 November 2002.

13. Michael Dell, interview by author, Boston, 5 April 2002.

14. Lafley interview.

15. Darrell Rigby and Chris Zook, "Open-Market Innovation," *Harvard Business Review,* October 2002: 80–89.

16. Gil Cloyd, interview by author, Boston, 26 July 2002.

17. C. K. Prahalad and Gary Hamel, "The Core Competence of the Corporation," *Harvard Business Review,* May 1990: 81.

Chapter 3: Evaluating Adjacency Moves

1. Christopher Gent, interview by author, London, 17 January 2003.

2. Julian Horn-Smith, interview by author, Boston, 4 February 2002.

3. Gary McWilliams and Ann Zimmerman, "Dell Plans to Peddle PCs Inside Sears, Other Large Chains—Kiosks Allow Customers to Try Out Computers Before Placing Orders; A Trojan Horse for New Printers?" *Wall Street Journal,* 30 January 2003.

4. The company pairs were selected for analysis of the role of adjacency strategies in performance because of various factors, such as industry similarity, degree of focus (not conglomerates), clearly different adjacency choices, different performance trajectories over a ten-year period, and publicly available data.

5. Ian McLaurin, interview by author, London, 26 November 2002.

6. Harlan S. Byrne, "Cardinal Distribution Inc.," *Barron's,* 11 November 1991, 47.

7. Ralph T. King Jr., "McKesson's Chairman, CEO, Five Others Step Down or Are Fired Amid Scandal," *Wall Street Journal,* 22 June 1999.

8. The concept of an industry profit pool is arguably as important as measuring the physical size of a market in units, yet relatively few market analyses by companies do this rigorously. Some of the best discussions of the profit pool or examples of companies that dramatically tilt the profit pool in their favor and discussions whose logic I have drawn on for this section are in Clayton Christensen, *The Innovator's Dilemma;* Adrian Slywotzky, *Value Migration;* Gary Hamel and C. K. Prahalad, *Competing for the Future;* and Orit Gadiesh and Jim Gilbert, "Profit Pools: A Fresh Look at Strategy," *Harvard Business Review,* May–June 1998, and "How to Map Your Industry's Profit Pool," *Harvard Business Review,* May–June 1998.

9. "Mayo's Lessons" (editorial comment), *Financial Times,* 21 January 2002.

10. Robert S. McNamara, *In Retrospect* (New York: Times Books, 1995), xvi.

11. Dave Lumley, interview by author, Boston, 13 March 2002.

12. Alecia Swasy, *Changing Focus* (New York: Random House Times Business, 1997), 13.

13. Pitman interview.

Chapter 4: Orchestrating Adjacency Moves

1. S. Davies et al., *The Dynamics of Market Leadership in the U.K. Manufacturing Industry, 1979–1986* (London: Centre for Business Strategy, 1991), 27.

2. Constantinos Markides, "Strategic Innovation," *Sloan Management Review,* spring 1997.

3. Frederick F. Reichheld, *The Loyalty Effect: The Hidden Force Behind Growth, Profits, and Lasting Value* (Boston: Harvard Business School Press, 1996), 67.

4. "Crunch at Chrysler," *The Economist,* 12 November 1994, 93.

5. Hal Sperlich, interview by author, Cleveland, 20 November 2002.

6. Ibid.

7. Alex Taylor III, "U.S. Cars Come Back," *Time,* 16 November 1992, 60.

8. Ibid., 52.

9. Bill Monahan, telephone interview by author, 12 July 2002.

10. Marcel Telles, interview by author, Boston, 13 June 2002.

11. M. Mitchell Waldrop, *Complexity: The Emerging Science at the Edge of Order and Chaos* (New York: Simon & Schuster, 1992), 30.

12. Emmanuel Kampouris, interview by author, New York, 9 July 2002.

13. William Carter, quoted in Carter's, internal publication, August 1990.

14. Fred Rowan, interview by author, Atlanta, 9 August 2002.

Chapter 5: Executing Adjacency Moves

1. Bain/EIU Survey, October 2002.

2. Dell interview.

3. Tim Eller, interview by author, Boston, 4 April 2002.

4. Taylor interview.

5. Fung interview.

6. Larry Hirsch, interview by author, Boston, 4 April 2002.

7. Stemberg interview.

8. Taylor interview.

9. Pistorio interview.

10. Telles interview.

11. Mike Eskew, interview by author, Atlanta, 9 August 2002.

12. Vincent interview.

13. Robert Burgelman and Andrew S. Grove, *Strategy Is Destiny* (New York: Simon & Schuster, 2001), 332.

14. Eskew interview.

15. Thomas S. Kuhn, *The Structure of Scientific Revolutions* (Chicago: University of Chicago Press, 1996).

16. Nick Shreiber, interview by author, Copenhagen, 28 May 2002.

17. Bain/EIU Survey, October 2002.

18. Taylor interview.

19. Monahan interview.

20. Shreiber interview.

21. Eller interview.

22. Andrew S. Grove, chairman and founder of Intel, panel discussion at Harvard Burning Questions Conference, San Jose, CA, 3 October 2002.

23. Royce Yudkoff, interview by author, Boston, 24 June 2002.

24. Jack Welch, Getting Back on Offense Conference, New York, 20 June 2002.

Chapter 6: Transforming Through Adjacency Moves

1. "How to Live Long and Prosper," *The Economist*, 10 May 1997, 59.

2. Hirsch interview.

3. Ibid.

4. Ibid.

5. David Liniger, interview by author, New York, 11 March 2003.

6. Joseph Franklin Wall, *The Andrew Carnegie Reader* (Pittsburgh: University of Pittsburgh Press, 1992), 50.

Bibliography

Books

Barabasi, Albert-Laszlo. *Linked: The New Science of Networks*. New York: Perseus Publishing, 2002.

Burgelman, Robert, and Andrew S. Grove, *Strategy Is Destiny*. New York: Simon & Schuster, 2001.

Burns, Stan. *Exceeding Expectations: The Enterprise Rent-A-Car Story*. Lyme, CT: Greenwich Publishing Group, 1997.

Carroll, Glenn R., and Michael T. Hannan. *The Demography of Corporations and Industries*. Princeton: Princeton University Press, 2000.

Chesbrough, Henry. *Open Innovation*. Boston: Harvard Business School Press, 2003.

Christensen, Clayton M. *The Innovator's Dilemma: When New Technologies Cause Great Firms to Fail*. Boston: Harvard Business School Press, 1997.

Collins, James C., and Jerry I. Porras. *Built to Last: Successful Habits of Visionary Companies*. New York: HarperBusiness, 1997.

Collins, Jim. *Good to Great*. New York: HarperBusiness, 2001.

Davies, S., et al. *The Dynamics of Market Leadership in the U.K. Manufacturing Industry, 1979–1986*. London: Centre for Business Strategy, 1991.

Dell, Michael, with Catherine Fredman. *Direct from Dell: Strategies That Revolutionized an Industry*. New York: HarperBusiness, 1999.

Dimson, Elroy, Paul Marsh, and Mike Staunton. *Triumph of the Optimists: 101 Years of Global Investment Returns*. Princeton: Princeton University Press, 2002.

Dyer, Davis, Frederick Dalzell, and Rowena Olegario. *Rising Tide*. Boston: Harvard Business School Press, 2004.

Gleick, James. *Chaos: Making a New Science*. New York: Penguin Books, 1987.

Gompers, Paul A., and Josh Lerner. *The Money of Invention: How Venture Capital Creates New Wealth*. Boston: Harvard Business School Press, 2001.

Halberstam, David, and John S. McCain. *The Best and the Brightest*. New York: Random House, 1993.

Hamel, Gary, and C. K. Prahalad. *Competing for the Future*. Boston: Harvard Business School Press, 1994.

Henderson, Bruce D. *Henderson on Corporate Strategy*. Cambridge: Abt Books, 1979.

Janus, Irving. *Groupthink*. Boston: Houghton Mifflin, 1982.

Jones, Steve. *Darwin's Ghost*. New York: Random House, 2000.

Katsenelinboigen, Aron. *Indeterministic Economics*. New York: Praeger Publishers, 1992.

Keegan, John. *A History of Warfare*. New York: Vintage Books, 1993.

Kuhn, Thomas S. *The Structure of Scientific Revolutions*. Chicago: University of Chicago Press, 1996.

Leander, Lars. *Tetra Pak: A Vision Becomes Reality*. Lund, Sweden: Tetra Pak Intl., Corporate Communications, 1995.

Lorsch, Jay W., and Thomas J. Tierney. *Aligning the Stars: How to Succeed When Professionals Drive Results*. Boston: Harvard Business School Press, 2002.

Massingill, Reed. *Becoming American Express*. New York: American Express Company, 1999.

McNamara, Robert S. *In Retrospect*. New York: Times Books, 1995.

Means, Howard B., and David Grubin. *Money and Power: The History of Business*. New York: John Wiley & Sons, 2001.

Nesheim, John. *High Tech Start Up*. New York: Free Press, 2000.

Porter, Michael E. *Competitive Advantage*. New York: Free Press, 1985.

Rappaport, Alfred, and Michael J. Mauboussin. *Expectations Investing: Reading Stock Prices for Better Returns*. Boston: Harvard Business School Press, 2001.

Reichheld, Frederick F. *Loyalty Rules!* Boston: Harvard Business School Press, 2001.

———. *The Loyalty Effect: The Hidden Force Behind Growth, Profits, and Lasting Value*. Boston: Harvard Business School Press, 1996.

Sampson, Curt. *Hogan*. Nashville, TN: Rutledge Hill Press, 2001.

Simon, Hermann. *Hidden Champions: Lessons from Five Hundred of the World's Best Unknown Companies*. Boston: Harvard Business School Press, 1996.

Sirower, Mark L. *The Synergy Trap: How Companies Lose the Acquisition Game*. New York: Free Press, 1997.

Slater, Robert. *Saving Big Blue: Leadership Lessons and Turnaround Tactics of IBM's Lou Gerstner.* New York: McGraw Hill, 1999.

Slywotzky, Adrian J. *Value Migration: How to Think Several Moves Ahead of the Competition.* Boston: Harvard Business School Press, 1995.

Smith, Adam. *The Money Game.* New York: Random House, 1976.

Sobel, Robert. *When Giants Stumble: Classic Business Blunders and How to Avoid Them.* New York: Prentice Hall Press, 1999.

Steinbock, Dan. *The Nokia Revolution: The Story of an Extraordinary Company That Transformed an Industry.* New York: AMACOM, 2001.

Stemberg, Thomas S. *Staples for Success.* Santa Monica, CA: Knowledge Exchange, 1996.

Stewart, G. Bennet III. *The Quest for Value.* New York: Stern Stewart, 1993.

Swasy, Alecia. *Changing Focus: Kodak and the Battle to Save a Great American Company.* New York: Random House Times Business, 1997.

Tellis, Gerard J., and Peter N. Golder. *Will and Vision: How Latecomers Grow to Dominate Markets.* New York: McGraw Hill, 2002.

Utterback, James M. *Mastering the Dynamics of Innovation.* Boston: Harvard Business School Press, 1994.

Vlasic, Bill, and Bradley Stertz. *Taken for a Ride.* New York: HarperCollins, 2000.

Von Hipple, Eric. *The Sources of Innovation.* New York: Oxford University Press, 1988.

Waldrop, M. Mitchell. *Complexity: The Emerging Science at the Edge of Order and Chaos.* New York: Simon & Schuster, 1992.

Wall, Joseph Franklin. *The Andrew Carnegie Reader.* Pittsburgh: University of Pittsburgh Press, 1992.

Zook, Chris, with James Allen. *Profit from the Core.* Boston: Harvard Business School Press, 2001.

Articles

Byrne, Harlan. "Cardinal Distribution Inc." *Barron's,* 11 November 1991.

Cornell, Bradford. "Is the Response of Analysts to Information Consistent with Fundamental Valuation? The Case of Intel." *Financial Management,* spring 2001.

"Crunch at Chrysler." *The Economist,* 12 November 1994.

Deutsche Bank. "Utilities and Their Telcos." *Equity Research,* November 2000.

Gadiesh, Orit, and James L. Gilbert. "How to Map Your Industry's Profit Pool." *Harvard Business Review,* May–June 1998.

———. "Profit Pools: A Fresh Look at Strategy." *Harvard Business Review,* May–June 1998.

Garvin, David A., and Artemis March. "Harvey Golub: Recharging American Express." Case 9-396-212. Boston: Harvard Business School, 1996.

Goldberg, Michael, and Justin Pettit. "The New Math: 4 > 8." *Stern Stewart Research Evaluation,* September 2000.

Hatfield, Louise, John Sleeth, Randall Pitts, and Michael Lyon. "Toward Validation of Partner Goal Achievement As a Measure of Joint Venture Performance." *Journal of Managerial Issues,* fall 1998.

Henry, David. "Mergers: Why Most Big Deals Don't Pay Off." *BusinessWeek,* 14 October 2002.

Herzberg, Martin M. "Implementing EBO/EVA Analysis in Stock Selection." *Journal of Investing,* spring 1998.

"How to Live Long and Prosper." *The Economist,* 10 May 1997.

King, Ralph T. Jr. "McKesson's Chairman, CEO, Five Others Step Down or Are Fired Amid Scandal." *Wall Street Journal,* 22 June 1999.

Lajoux, Alexandra, and Fred Weston. "Do Deals Deliver on Postmerger Performance?: A Summary of McKinsey (1987), Mercer/Business Week (1995) and Kenneth Smith Studies." *Mergers and Acquisitions,* September–October 1998.

Lanes, Kersten, and Richard Stewart. "What the Stock Market Wants to Know About a Merger: A Summary of Price WaterhouseCoopers (2001) Study." *Mergers and Acquisitions,* May 2001.

Lowenstein, Roger. "Goldman Study of Stocks' Rise in the '80s Poses a Big Riddle." *Wall Street Journal,* 6 June 1991.

Luehrman, Timothy A. "Using APV: A Better Tool for Valuing Operations." *Harvard Business Review,* May–June 1997.

Luzi, Michael, and Gregor Matthies. "Business Europe: Bland's Dilemma at BT." *Wall Street Journal Europe,* 7 May 2001.

Mandel, Michael. "The Painful Truth About Profits." *BusinessWeek,* 4 November 2002.

Markides, Constantinos C. "Strategic Innovation." *Sloan Management Review,* spring 1997.

Masud, Sam. "Mega Deals, Mega Risks: A Summary of A. T. Kearney (1998) Study." *Telecommunications,* March 1999.

"Mayo's Lessons." Editorial comment. *Financial Times,* 21 January 2002.

McWilliams, Gary, and Ann Zimmerman. "Dell Plans to Peddle PCs Inside Sears, Other Large Chains." *Wall Street Journal,* 30 January 2003.

Miles, Richard. "Lloyds TSB." *Times,* 10 November 1997.

Osborne, Richard. "New Product Development—Lesser Royals." *Industry Week,* 1 April 2002.

Prahalad, C. K., and Gary Hamel. "The Core Competence of the Corporation." *Harvard Business Review,* May–June 1990.

Putnam, Blu. "The US Is More Like an Emerging Market." *Global Investor,* May 2000.

Rigby, Darrell, and Chris Zook. "Open-Market Innovation." *Harvard Business Review,* October 2002.

Schuler, Randall, and Susan Jackson. "HR Issues and Activities in Mergers and Acquisitions: A Summary of Lehman Brothers Study." *European Management Journal,* June 2001.

Taylor, Alex III. "U.S. Cars Come Back." *Time,* 16 November 1992.

Tetenbaum, Tony. "Beating the Odds of Merger and Acquisition Failure: Seven Key Practices That Improve the Chance for Expected Integration and Synergies: A Summary of Mark Sirower's 'The Synergy Trap.'" *Organizational Dynamics,* autumn 1999.

Yook, Ken C., and George M. McCabe. "MVA and the Cross-Section of Expected Stock Returns." *Journal of Portfolio Management,* spring 2001.

Index

About the Author

CHRIS ZOOK is a director at Bain & Company, a global management consulting firm focused on making companies more valuable. He heads the company's Global Strategy Practice and is a member of Bain's Management Committee and Investment Committee.

During his 20 years at Bain, Zook's work has focused on companies searching for new sources of profitable growth, in a wide range of industries. This work led to the writing of his best-selling business book, *Profit from the Core* (Harvard Business School Press, 2001). *Profit from the Core* provides a blueprint to finding new sources of growth from a core business, based on a three-year study of thousands of companies worldwide. Its findings are being implemented in many successful companies worldwide.

Mr. Zook has written extensively in the business press, is a frequent guest on television and radio, and has spoken at many esteemed business forums. He received a B.A. from Williams College, an M.Phil. in Economics from Exeter College, Oxford University, and holds Master's and Ph.D. degrees from Harvard University.